Submersible Tales

Submersible Tales

TITAN'S OCEANIC EXPLORATION

Mack Rafeal

Spectra Enterprise

Contents

Table of Content

Introduction: The Call of Titan's Depths

5.1 Titan Voyager reaches the surface of Titan's ocean.

5.2 Initial discoveries and challenges as the submersible begins its descent into the abyss.

5.3 Encounter with unique and unexpected life forms in Titan's dark waters.

Chapter 6: Unveiling Titan's Secrets

6.1 Exploration of Titan's underwater landscape and geological features.

6.2 The team uncovers clues about the moon's history and evolution.

6.3 Scientific breakthroughs and surprises that challenge previous assumptions.

Chapter 7: Deep-Sea Drama

7.1 Unexpected challenges and dangers arise as Titan Voyager explores deeper.

7.2 Technical malfunctions, encounters with hostile creatures, and the resilience of the team in overcoming crises.

7.3 The emotional toll on the crew as they face the unknown.

Chapter 8: The Abyssal Gateway

8.1 The team discovers a mysterious underwater gateway leading to uncharted depths.

8.2 Ethical dilemmas and debates about whether to venture into the unknown.

8.3 The decision to explore the gateway and the potential consequences.

Chapter 9: Beyond the Abyss

9.1 The team ventures beyond the abyssal gateway into unexplored regions of Titan's ocean.

9.2 A culmination of discoveries, challenges, and the team's ultimate mission objectives.

9.3 The conclusion of the mission and the impact of Titan's exploration on our understanding of extraterrestrial oceans.

Introduction

The Call of Titan's Depths

In the tremendous region of our nearby planet group, in the midst of the whirling grandiose artful dance, one heavenly body has long enraptured the creative mind of researchers and visionaries the same - Titan, Saturn's biggest moon. Titan, with its thick orange environment and freezing temperatures, presents a supernatural charm that allures investigation and sparkles the human soul of interest. This mysterious moon, covered in secret and interest, has turned into a point of convergence for logical request and hypothesis about the potential for extraterrestrial life.

As we set out on the excursion to comprehend Titan's profundities, we are defied with a bunch of inquiries that stretch out past the limits of our ongoing information. What lies underneath its thick climate? Might Titan at some point hold onto the structure blocks of life? These inquiries reverberate with the very interest that energized the space race and keep on driving our investigation of the universe.

One of Titan's most striking highlights is its thick environment, made essentially out of nitrogen with hints of methane and ethane. This extraordinary mix gives Titan an orange tone and hides its surface from direct perception. The craving to puncture this cloak and reveal the insider facts concealed underneath Titan's climatic cover has prompted a progression of aggressive missions and recommendations.

NASA's Cassini-Huygens mission, which investigated the Saturn framework from 2004 to 2017, gave significant experiences into Titan's air and surface. The Huygens test slipped through Titan's environment, uncovering a different scene with immense sand ridges, frosty fields, and fluid methane lakes. These revelations just developed the interest encompassing Titan and energized the journey to dig further into its profundities.

One of the critical inspirations for investigating Titan lies in the chance of finding conditions helpful for life. While Titan's surface is aloof to Earth-based life, its subsurface sea - guessed to exist underneath its cold outside - raises the tempting possibility of livable conditions. The revelation of fluid water on other heavenly bodies has for some time been viewed as a vital calculate the quest for extraterrestrial life, and Titan's subsurface sea adds another aspect to this mission.

As we consider the likely tenability of Titan, mainstream researchers is as of now formulating missions to open the mysteries of its profundities. Ideas like the Titan Saturn Framework Mission (TSSM) and the Titan Female horse Traveler (TiME) mean to additionally investigate Titan's surface and subsurface, disentangling the secrets that falsehood concealed underneath layers of ice and methane. These missions address the following wilderness in our journey to figure out the circumstances important for life past Earth.

Past the logical inspirations, the investigation of Titan likewise holds guarantee for propelling comprehension we might interpret planetary cycles and the arrangement of divine bodies. Titan's remarkable geography, formed by processes unmistakable from those on The planet, presents a chance to expand our insight into planetary advancement. By concentrating on Titan, researchers desire to acquire experiences into the mind boggling exchange of geographical, air, and hydrological processes that shape the surfaces of far off universes.

Besides, Titan fills in as a proving ground for creative advancements that might be critical for future space investigation tries. The outrageous circumstances on Titan's surface, with its low temperatures and thick environment, require specific hardware and designing arrangements. Creating and testing these advancements on Titan progresses how we might interpret this moon as well as sets us up for the difficulties of investigating other frigid bodies in our planetary group and then some.

The charm of Titan reaches out past the domain of science and innovation; it reverberates with a crucial human intuition - the inclination to investigate the unexplored world. Titan, with its puzzling lakes and immense regions, inspires a feeling of marvel and experience that rises above logical request. The call of Titan's profundities repeats the memorable excursions of investigation that have molded how we might interpret the world and the universe.

As we stand on the cliff of another time of room investigation, with plans for ran missions to the Moon and Mars coming to fruition, Titan arises as a convincing objective for human investigation. The possibility of people going to this far off moon, with its ethereal scenes and expected livable conditions, lights the creative mind and welcomes us to consider a future where Titan assumes a focal part in our investigation of the universe.

1. **Introduction to the mysterious moon Titan and its enigmatic ocean.**
   In the huge embroidery of our planetary group, where divine bodies dance in the grandiose expressive dance, one moon stands apart as an enrapturing mystery - Titan, the biggest moon of Saturn. Shrouded in an environment thicker than that of Earth and flaunting a different scene, Titan has long provoked the interest of cosmologists, researchers, and space lovers. In any case, past the noticeable surface lies a secret domain that has turned into the focal point of extraordinary

logical hypothesis - Titan's perplexing sea.

The excursion to comprehend Titan's secrets starts with its particular environment, a cover of nitrogen encompassing the moon and bestowing an orange shade. This thick climate, made essentially out of nitrogen with hints of methane and ethane, has protected Titan's surface from direct perception for a really long time. It was only after the coming of cutting edge space investigation missions that we acquired a brief look into the insider facts held by this puzzling moon.

NASA's Cassini-Huygens mission, a cooperative exertion with the European Space Organization (ESA), left on a noteworthy investigation of the Saturn framework from 2004 to 2017. The mission's discoveries gave uncommon bits of knowledge into Titan's climate as well as made way for a more profound comprehension of its surface and secret profundities. The Huygens test, let out of the Cassini shuttle, plummeted through Titan's air, uncovering a world that blew some minds.

Titan's surface, as uncovered by Huygens, is a scene of limits - huge sand hills, sweeping frosty fields, and fluid methane lakes dabbing the scene. This variety indicated complex topographical and hydrological processes forming the moon's surface. Notwithstanding, it was the disclosure of Titan's potential subsurface sea that additional a layer of interest to the investigation.

Underneath the frigid outside that covers Titan lies the tempting chance of a subsurface sea, a domain of fluid water stowed away from direct perception. The presence of a sea on Titan brings up issues about its piece, profundity, and the potential for livability. Might this outsider sea at any point hold onto the vital elements forever, or is it a cold, unwelcoming field? The solutions to these inquiries stay subtle, yet the quest for information drives logical request forward.

Mainstream researchers' advantage in Titan's sea is powered by the more extensive mission for extraterrestrial life. While Titan's surface circumstances are brutal and unwelcoming, the subsurface sea presents a better climate for life to flourish possibly. The quest for fluid water on other heavenly bodies has for quite some time been a point of convergence in the investigation of our planetary group, and Titan's sea adds another aspect to this journey.

As we ponder the secrets of Titan's sea, proposition and mission ideas are arising to dig further into this unfamiliar domain. The Titan Saturn Framework Mission (TSSM) and the Titan Horse Wayfarer (TiME) are among the missions imagined to investigate Titan's surface and examine the properties of its sea. These missions address the following section in our continuous investigation of Titan and hold the possibility to open the mysteries of this baffling moon.

Past the logical inspirations, the investigation of Titan's sea likewise meets with how we might interpret planetary cycles and the arrangement of heavenly bodies. Titan's remarkable geographical elements, formed by a blend of natural science and climatic cooperations, offer a brief look into the unpredictable dance of powers that shape planetary scenes. Concentrating on Titan's sea gives a window into the more extensive cycles that have molded our planetary group north of billions of years.

Besides, Titan fills in as a proving ground for state of the art advances that push the limits of human development. The outrageous circumstances on Titan's surface - with temperatures plunging to short 290 degrees Fahrenheit (less 179 degrees Celsius) and a thick environment - request particular hardware and designing arrangements. Creating and testing these innovations on Titan progresses how we might interpret this moon as well as sets us up for the difficulties of investigating other frosty bodies in our nearby planet group and then some.

While the logical and innovative parts of Titan's investigation are convincing, there is likewise a significant human component to the journey. Titan, with its ethereal excellence and the charm of the obscure, allures us to investigate past the restrictions of our ongoing comprehension. The call to disentangle the mysteries of Titan's sea reverberates with the very soul of investigation that has driven humankind to wander into the obscure since forever ago.

As we stand on the cusp of another time of room investigation, with goals to return people to the Moon and excursion forward to Mars, Titan arises as an objective that catches the creative mind. The possibility of human investigation of Titan's confounding sea is certainly not a far off dream yet a substantial objective that could reshape how we might interpret the universe. Envisioning space explorers testing the profundities of an outsider sea, clad in cutting edge spacesuits, brings out a feeling of miracle and fervor that rises above the limits of our ebb and flow mechanical capacities.

2. **The protagonist, Dr. Olivia Hayes, receives a groundbreaking mission to explore Titan's ocean using a state-of-the-art submersible.**

Dr. Olivia Hayes remained in the faintly lit control room of the space organization's base camp, her eyes fixed on the holographic projection of Titan drifting in the air before her. The air was accused of expectation as she consumed the subtleties of the momentous mission that had recently been alloted to her - an endeavor to investigate the secretive sea concealed underneath the frosty hull of Saturn's biggest moon.

As the lead researcher and head agent, Dr. Hayes had devoted her profession to planetary investigation, yet this mission was unique. It wasn't just about concentrating on Titan from a good ways; it was tied in with diving into the obscure profundities of an outsider sea. The excitement of disclosure blended with a hint of fear as she examined the difficulties that lay ahead.

The mission, named Titan Sea Pilgrim (TOE), was imagined as a coordinated effort between numerous space organizations, pooling assets and mastery to open the insider facts of Titan's cryptic sea. Dr. Hayes, known for her spearheading work in astrobiology and planetary geography, was handpicked to lead the mission. Her standing as a brave pioneer and her capacity to explore the intricacies of extraterrestrial conditions made her the best contender for this uncommon endeavor.

The core of the TOE mission was a cutting edge submarine intended to endure the outrageous states of Titan's sea. The submarine, named Aquarius, addressed the zenith of mechanical development. Its smooth, titanium-combination outline housed a set-up of logical instruments equipped for breaking down the creation of the sea's profundities, planning the territory, and catching high-goal pictures. Aquarius was not only a vessel; it was a versatile research center, prepared to lead an exhaustive assessment of Titan's submerged world.

As Dr. Hayes really got to know the subtleties of the mission, a blend of fervor and obligation settled inside her. The possibility of being the principal human to investigate an extraterrestrial sea was striking, yet it likewise conveyed the heaviness of logical assumptions and the potential for pivotal revelations that could reshape how we might interpret life past Earth.

The excursion to Titan was not a simple bounce across the nearby planet group. It required cautious preparation, exact route, and the coordination of various space apparatus. The send off window was painstakingly determined to guarantee that Aquarius would show up at Titan with pinpoint precision. As the mission commencement initiated, Dr. Hayes really wanted to feel a feeling of fate - a combination of her labor of love and the chance to spearhead another period of investigation.

The shuttle bringing Aquarius rushed through the void of room, its direction set for Saturn's biggest moon. The excursion, however estimated in galactic units, felt like a jump into the unexplored world. Dr. Hayes and her group checked the space apparatus' advancement with a combination of expectation and apprehensive energy. The progress of the mission relied upon the faultless execution of each stage - from the underlying send off to the orbital inclusion around Titan.

After arriving at Titan's circle, the space apparatus sent Aquarius, and the sub isolated from its interplanetary transporter. As Aquarius dropped through Titan's air, the thick orange fog bit by bit encompassed the sub. The shuttle's sensors and cameras enacted, catching the primary looks at Titan's surface as it plummeted toward the frigid hull that covered the sea beneath.

The section into Titan's sea was a fragile dance, an artful dance of engines and stabilizers as Aquarius explored through the frigid layers. At last, with a delicate sprinkle, the sub connected with the fluid surface, making swells that reverberated through the cold sea. Dr. Hayes, watching the live feed from the control room, felt a flood of elation as Aquarius sunk into the outsider climate.

The primary errand was to direct a progression of starter sweeps and evaluations. Aquarius' sensors murmured to life, catching information on temperature, pressure, and the synthetic structure of the sea.

The pictures communicated back to Earth showed a dreamlike submerged scene - cold developments looking like lowered mountains and valleys, washed in an extraordinary sparkle. It was a sight that no human had at any point seen, and Dr.

Hayes couldn't resist the opportunity to wonder about the magnificence of Titan's secret world.

As the investigation proceeded, Aquarius dove further into the sea's profundities. The sub's high level sonar frameworks planned the geography of the sea depths, uncovering huge fields and startling geographical elements. Dr. Hayes and her group were charmed by the variety of the submerged territory, hypothesizing on the powers that had formed Titan's maritime scene over ages.

One of the essential targets of the mission was to gather tests from the sea floor. Aquarius was furnished with a mechanical arm equipped for gathering up dregs and frosty hull tests. These examples held the way to figuring out the sythesis of Titan's sea and the potential forever. Dr. Hayes watched anxiously as the mechanical arm expanded, carefully gathering tests that would be fixed and put away for the excursion back to Earth.

The information spilling in from Aquarius portrayed Titan's sea. The synthetic investigation uncovered a combination of water and hydrocarbons, with hints of natural mixtures. The temperature and strain conditions were cruel by all accounts, yet the presence of fluid water and natural particles indicated the chance of livable zones inside Titan's profundities. Mainstream researchers on Earth enthusiastically anticipated the itemized examinations that would continue in the months to come.

As the mission advanced, Aquarius experienced surprising peculiarities. Abnormal flows and whirlpools indicated dynamic cycles inside the sea - maybe determined by flowing powers applied by Saturn's gravitational force. Dr. Hayes and her group changed the submarine's direction to explore these abnormalities, perceiving the significance of understanding the sea's elements in unwinding the secrets of Titan.

The correspondence delay among Earth and Titan added a component of tension to the mission. Each order shipped off Aquarius assumed control more than an hour to arrive at the submarine, and the resulting information and pictures required a comparable span for transmission back to Earth. The control room hummed with expectation during these times of delaying, as researchers and architects enthusiastically anticipated the unfurling story of Titan's maritime investigation.

As Aquarius proceeded with its submerged excursion, the mission's importance resounded across established researchers and the general population at large. The pictures and information communicated from Titan caught the aggregate creative mind, igniting conversations about the potential for life past Earth and the tremendous conceivable outcomes concealed inside our planetary group.

Dr. Hayes ended up at the focal point of a logical and social peculiarity, adjusting the obligations of a spearheading traveler with the heaviness of public assumptions.

The mission's prosperity wasn't without challenges. Aquarius confronted specialized misfires, unexpected impediments, and the consistent strain of working in an outrageous climate. However, the flexibility of the sub and the commitment of the mission group won. Each challenge turned into a learning a potential open door, adding to the general progress of the mission and fortifying humankind's ability to investigate far off universes.

As Aquarius started its climb back to the surface, weighed down with tests and a stash of logical information, the feeling of achievement in the control room was unmistakable. Dr. Hayes, remaining among her associates, pondered the excursion from the origination of the mission to the acknowledgment of its goals. The investigation of Titan's sea had not just extended how we might interpret this far off moon yet had likewise prepared for future missions and the proceeded with look for life past Earth.

The return excursion to Earth denoted the finish of the Titan Sea Pioneer mission. The rocket conveying Aquarius reemerged Earth's environment, carrying with it the climax of long periods of arranging, development, and investigation. The recuperation group anxiously anticipated the sub's recovery, anxious to analyze the examples that held the privileged insights of Titan's sea inside their frozen centers.

Dr. Once more olivia Hayes, remaining in the control room, looked as Aquarius was painstakingly lifted from the rocket and moved to the anticipating researchers. The examples were exposed to a battery of examinations, and the discoveries, when delivered to general society, lighted a reestablished feeling of miracle and interest in the universe.

The investigation of Titan's sea had extended the boondocks of human information as well as enlivened another age of researchers, designers, and visionaries. Dr. Hayes, presently viewed as a trailblazer in planetary investigation, planned ahead with confidence. The secrets of Titan were only the start, and as mankind's venture broadened farther into the universe, the call of the obscure kept on reverberating across the immeasurability of room. The Titan Sea Voyager mission had demonstrated that the human soul of investigation, furnished with state of the art innovation and logical interest, could open the mysteries of even the most confounding universes in our nearby planet group.

Chapter 1

The Team Assembles

The expectation lingered palpably like a charged current as the group assembled in the war room, a best in class office intended to work with the most unpredictable and aggressive investigations. It was a pivotal event - the perfection of long stretches of arranging, readiness, and relentless commitment. The Submarine Stories Titan's Maritime Investigation was going to begin, and the group, a different gathering of specialists from different logical disciplines, remained on the cliff of an excursion into the unexplored world.

In charge of this amphibian odyssey was Dr. Victoria Hayes, a famous sea life researcher and the visionary behind the Sub Stories project. Her energy for the sea's secrets was matched exclusively by her mastery in sea life science. Dr. Hayes, with her puncturing look and a disposition that radiated certainty, tended to the collected group with a combination of energy and assurance. Her administration set the vibe for the impending endeavor, underscoring the significance of joint effort and the quest for information that rose above disciplinary limits.

The group, a mosaic of ability, included oceanographers, geologists, marine specialists, roboticists, and prepared submariners. Every part offered a one of a kind arrangement of abilities and encounters of real value, framing an aggregate knowledge that would demonstrate fundamental in exploring the difficulties of the remote ocean.

As the gathering presented themselves, the room hummed with a substantial energy, a common excitement for the exceptional experience that looked for them.

Leader James Mitchell, a veteran submariner with many years of involvement exploring the deep profundities, would be at the controls of the Sub Stories Titan. His steely look and quiet disposition mirrored a certainty brought into the world of incalculable hours spent underneath the waves. Mitchell's skill in steering submarines was a foundation of the mission's prosperity, guaranteeing the protected plummet and climb of the Titan even with the outrageous tensions that looked for them.

Close by him was Dr. Emily Chang, a geologist enthusiastically for disentangling the insider facts of the World's outside. Outfitted with a sharp eye for detail and a significant comprehension of structural cycles, Dr. Chang intended to gather tests from the sea floor that would offer important bits of knowledge into the land history of the seabed. Her geologic aptitude was supplemented by the state of the art apparatuses and scientific instruments on board the Titan.

The group's innovative spine was Dr. Alan Rodriguez, a roboticist liable for directing the sending and activity of the submarine's mechanical arms. These arms, outfitted with high-goal cameras and able controllers, were fundamental for catching examples, directing tests, and archiving the rich woven artwork of marine life that anticipated revelation. Dr. Rodriguez's authority of mechanical technology would demonstrate instrumental in opening the secrets of the remote ocean.

As the colleagues shared their experiences, it became obvious that the progress of the Submarine Stories Titan's Maritime Investigation depended on the consistent coordination of their different aptitude. Dr. Marcus Thompson, a sea life researcher having some expertise in bioluminescent organic entities, examined his energy about concentrating on the special variations of life in the remote ocean. His energy was infectious, igniting a feeling of miracle among his partners as they pondered the potential disclosures looking for them in the chasm.

The environmental control room, a center of movement with its banks of screens and control boards, woke up as the group dived more deeply into the complexities of the Titan's tasks. The pressure in the room was tempered by a common feeling of direction - the quest for information and the longing to push the limits of human getting it. Dr. Hayes, remaining at the front of the war room, enunciated the meaning of their main goal and the obligation they bore as stewards of the sea's privileged insights.

As the group collected around a holographic presentation of the Submarine Stories Titan, they wondered about the mechanical wonder before them. The Titan, with its smoothed out plan and high level capacities, addressed the apex of human accomplishment in submerged investigation. It was a vessel that would convey them into the obscure, a signal of human resourcefulness that vowed to reveal the secrets disguised in the sea's profundities.

With the group completely collected and the Titan prepared for organization, the commencement to investigation started. The air in the war room thickened with a blend of fervor and expectation as the group ready for the earth shattering plunge. Dr. Hayes, her eyes mirroring a mix of assurance and wonder, expressed the words that reverberated through the room, "Let the investigation start."

As the Sub Stories Titan left on its maritime odyssey, the group's aggregate ability, energy, and brotherhood shaped the bedrock of this spearheading mission. The excursion into the profundities was not only a logical undertaking; it was a demonstration of the unyielding human soul, the tireless quest for information, and the significant association we share with the strange world that lies underneath the waves. The group, limited by a typical reason, wandered into the void with a feeling of worship for the neglected and a promise to disentangling the privileged insights of the sea - an excursion that would make a permanent imprint on the records of marine investigation.

1.1 Dr. Hayes assembles a diverse team of scientists, engineers, and explorers.

In the underlying phases of arranging the Sub Stories Titan's Maritime Investigation, Dr. Victoria Hayes, an illuminating presence in the field of sea life science, perceived the intricacy and greatness of the endeavor. Driven by a persevering interest in the secrets disguised underneath the sea's surface, she set out on the errand of gathering a group that could match the monstrosity of the mission. Dr. Hayes was not simply searching for specialists in a solitary field however looked for a multidisciplinary troupe that could handle the bunch difficulties of remote ocean investigation.

The primary expansion to the group was Commandant James Mitchell, a carefully prepared submariner whose abundance of involvement with exploring the sea's profundities made him a key resource. With a quiet disposition and a dominance of submarine tasks, Mitchell would expect the essential job of guiding the Sub Stories Titan, guaranteeing the wellbeing and accuracy expected for the endeavor's prosperity. Dr. Hayes perceived that the excursion into the obscure requested a pioneer with Mitchell's skill to explore the difficulties of the deep profundities.

To supplement Mitchell's seamanship, Dr. Hayes enrolled the gifts of Dr. Emily Chang, a recognized geologist work in the complicated cycles that shape the World's hull. Dr. Chang's ability would be urgent in unraveling the geographical secrets of the sea depths. She would lead the work to gather tests, unwind the historical backdrop of the seabed, and add to how we might interpret the powerful powers molding the submerged scene. The joining of topography into the campaign reflected Dr. Hayes' obligation to complete investigation.

Perceiving the significance of state of the art innovation in the progress of the mission, Dr. Hayes brought on board Dr. Alan Rodriguez, a splendid roboticist with a demonstrated history in creating progressed submerged mechanical frameworks. The Titan's mechanical arms, outfitted with high-goal cameras and accuracy instruments, would be under Dr. Rodriguez's order. His job was not just specialized; it was instrumental in guaranteeing that the Titan could associate with the remote ocean climate, gather information, and direct analyses with unmatched precision.

The group kept on growing with the expansion of experts from different logical disciplines, each picked for their extraordinary commitments to the exhaustive investigation of the sea. Dr. Marcus Thompson, a sea life scientist eminent for his investigations on bioluminescent creatures, carried a priceless point of view to the group. His interest with the variations of life in the remote ocean alluded to the potential for pivotal revelations that could reshape how we might interpret sea life science.

As the group gathered, the variety of mastery became evident. Oceanographers, specialists, researcher, and submariners met up, shaping an aggregate insight that rose above the limits of individual disciplines. Dr. Hayes, at the focal point of this assorted gathering, underlined the significance of joint effort and cooperative energy. The progress of the Sub Stories Titan's Maritime Investigation laid not just in the capability of each colleague however on their capacity to work strongly, utilizing their differed abilities to face the difficulties that looked for them in the profundities.

The war room, where the group gathered for briefings and arrangements, hummed with a mixture of energy, expectation, and centered assurance. Dr. Hayes, with a sharp feeling of initiative, explained the meaning of their main goal. She highlighted the obligation they bore as pilgrims wandering into the obscure and stewards of the sea's privileged insights. Her words resounded with the group, ingraining a feeling of direction that outperformed individual desires - an aggregate obligation to unwinding the secrets concealed underneath the waves.

The Submarine Stories Titan, a designing wonder intended to endure the outrageous states of the remote ocean, turned into the point of convergence of the group's consideration. Dr. Hayes, with a deep satisfaction and confidence, featured the mechanical progressions that would empower the Titan to catch extraordinary pictures, gather important information, and make ready for logical forward leaps.

The submarine was not only a vessel; it was an entrance to the obscure, a channel for human investigation into a domain that had escaped understanding for a really long time.

As the group got to know the complexities of the Titan, a substantial feeling of brotherhood arose. The cooperative soul that Dr. Hayes had looked to develop started to prosper as colleagues traded thoughts, tried gear, and calibrated their techniques. In this powerful climate, the different foundations of the researchers and designers ended up being a resource as opposed to a test, as every part offered an extraordinary viewpoint and set of abilities that would be useful.

The air in the war room was accused of a blend of fervor and apprehensive energy as the snapshot of organization drew closer. Dr. Hayes, remaining at the front, emanated certainty and assurance. The group, a mosaic of gifts and skill, was a demonstration of her vision of gathering a gathering that could by and large push the limits of human investigation.

As the Sub Stories Titan arranged for its plummet into the deep profundities, the group's solidarity turned out to be considerably more clear. Officer Mitchell, at the controls, imparted consistently with Dr. Chang, who was regulating the topographical parts of the mission. Dr. Rodriguez guaranteed that the automated arms were adjusted for ideal execution, while Dr. Thompson and the sea life researcher anxiously expected the disclosures that looked for them underneath the waves.

The excursion into the obscure had authoritatively started. Dr. Hayes, noticing the organized endeavors of her group, felt a significant feeling of satisfaction and obligation. The Sub Stories Titan's Maritime Investigation was not just a logical undertaking; it was a demonstration of the human soul's unquenchable hunger for information and the cooperative exertion expected to push the limits of investigation. The group, under Dr. Hayes' initiative, set out on a noteworthy mission to unwind the secrets of the remote ocean, furnished with an aggregate skill that vowed to reclassify how we might interpret the World's last boondocks.

1.2 Introduce key team members and their unique expertise.

As the Sub Stories Titan's Maritime Investigation left on its noteworthy excursion into the profundities of the sea, the outcome of the mission depended on the aggregate ability of its key colleagues. Dr. Victoria Hayes, the visionary head of the undertaking, cautiously organized a group of different gifts, each carrying a one of a kind arrangement of abilities to disentangle the secrets of the remote ocean.

At the very front of the group was Dr. Victoria Hayes herself, an illuminator in the field of sea life science.

With a significant enthusiasm for the sea and an immovable obligation to logical disclosure, Dr. Hayes filled in as both the main impetus behind the campaign and its directing visionary. Her broad information on marine biological systems, combined with a well established interest, set the vibe for the whole mission. Dr. Hayes was the orchestrator of the group as well as an involved researcher, anxious to dive into the obscure close by her partners.

Leader James Mitchell, a carefully prepared submariner with many years of involvement exploring the world's seas, expected a critical job in the outcome of the endeavor. His quiet disposition, sharpened through long stretches of directing subs in testing conditions, gave a consistent hand in charge of the Sub Stories Titan. Leader Mitchell's skill in sub activities was unmatched, and his capacity to explore the complex and frequently misleading states of the remote ocean was essential for the security and accuracy of the mission.

Dr. Emily Chang, a recognized geologist, added a critical aspect to the group's aggregate skill. Having some expertise in the investigation of Earth's hull and structural cycles, Dr. Chang was entrusted with disentangling the geographical secrets of the sea floor. Her sharp eye for rock developments and her capacity to decipher the unpretentious signs concealed in the seabed vowed to contribute priceless experiences into the geologic history of the remote ocean. Dr. Chang's work was central to understanding the powers molding the submerged scene and giving an extensive perspective on the sea's insider facts.

The innovative spine of the campaign was Dr. Alan Rodriguez, a splendid roboticist enthusiastically for creating progressed submerged mechanical frameworks. His skill in the plan and activity of the Titan's automated arms, furnished with high-goal cameras and accuracy instruments, was instrumental in the progress of the mission. Dr. Rodriguez's job reached out past the specialized viewpoints; he was entrusted with guaranteeing that the mechanical arms could communicate flawlessly with the remote ocean climate, permitting the group to gather tests, direct examinations, and record the rich biodiversity of the sea depths.

Dr. Marcus Thompson, a prestigious sea life researcher having some expertise in bioluminescent living beings, carried a special viewpoint to the group. His interest with the transformations of life in the remote ocean alluded to the potential for weighty disclosures that could reshape how we might interpret sea life science. Dr. Thompson's skill was especially significant given the Titan's high level capacities to investigate the most obscure corners of the sea, where bioluminescence assumed a critical part in the biology of remote ocean organic entities.

The coordinated effort between these key colleagues displayed the interdisciplinary idea of the campaign. As they assembled in the war room, a center point of mechanical complexity and logical expectation, the collaboration among the different gifts was obvious.

Dr. Hayes, with her capacity to connect the holes between logical disciplines, underscored the significance of aggregate knowledge in defying the difficulties that lay ahead.

In the war room, Dr. Hayes started briefings that featured the singular jobs of each colleague, encouraging a climate of open correspondence and cooperation. Commandant Mitchell, with an abundance of involvement, shared experiences into the functional parts of the sub, specifying the conventions for safe drop and rising into the deep profundities. Dr. Chang talked about the topographical targets, framing the particular locales of interest for test assortment and examination.

Dr. Rodriguez, encompassed by screens showing the Titan's mechanical arms, made sense of the complexities of their plan and usefulness. His show enlightened the mechanical arms' ability to explore the difficult states of the remote ocean and exhibited their adaptability in associating with the climate. The innovative wonder that Dr. Rodriguez had contributed was a demonstration of the combination of state of the art designing and logical investigation.

Dr. Thompson, the sea life scientist, gave an enamoring outline of the potential organic miracles anticipating revelation. His show included pictures and film from past remote ocean investigations, displaying the variety of life that flourished in the unforgiving states of the sea profundities. Dr. Thompson's excitement for uncovering the insider facts of bioluminescent organic entities reverberated with the whole group, touching off a common feeling of miracle.

As the group prepared for sending, the kinship among the key individuals turned out to be significantly more clear. Leader Mitchell, at the controls of the Submarine Stories Titan, kept a created center as he spoke with Dr. Chang, who firmly observed the plummet cycle. Dr. Rodriguez guaranteed that the automated arms were aligned for ideal execution, prepared to flawlessly execute the arranged assignments. Dr. Thompson and the sea life scholars enthusiastically expected the second when the Titan would arrive at the profundities, anxious to observe the secret domains that had escaped human perception.

The excursion into the pit denoted a notable second for each colleague and the aggregate undertaking overall. Dr. Hayes, remaining in the war room, noticed the cooperative endeavors with a significant feeling of satisfaction. The Sub Stories Titan's Maritime Investigation was not only a logical mission; it was a demonstration of human resourcefulness, investigation, and the voracious interest that had driven people to wander into the obscure since the beginning of time.

The sending of the Submarine Stories Titan into the deep profundities denoted the start of a groundbreaking investigation. As the group's one of a kind mastery joined in this undertaking, the potential for notable disclosures lingered not too far off.

The collaboration among Dr. Hayes, Leader Mitchell, Dr. Chang, Dr. Rodriguez, and Dr. Thompson exemplified the force of cooperative investigation, displaying the limit of human creativity to open the privileged insights concealed underneath the waves. The Submarine Stories Titan's Maritime Investigation, directed by this exceptional group, guaranteed not exclusively to grow how we might interpret the sea yet in addition to motivate people in the future to proceed with the journey for information in the strange and amazing profundities of the World's last wilderness.

1.3 Team dynamics and initial challenges in preparing for the unprecedented journey.

The Sub Stories Titan's Maritime Investigation, while powered by the aggregate mastery of its different group, was not without its underlying difficulties and the requirement for a finely tuned group dynamic. As the group ready for the phenomenal excursion into the remote ocean, the multifaceted exchange of characters, abilities, and cooperative endeavors became pivotal in exploring the intricacies of the mission.

In the beginning phases, the group elements were much the same as a painstakingly organized ensemble. Dr. Victoria Hayes, with her initiative intuition and profound comprehension of sea life science, filled in as the orchestrator, directing every part's commitments toward an amicable entirety. Her capacity to connect the holes between logical teaches and encourage cooperation established the groundwork for a durable group dynamic. Dr. Hayes perceived that the outcome of the campaign depended on individual ability as well as on the collaboration that arose when various gifts were united.

Officer James Mitchell, the veteran submariner, assumed a urgent part in forming the group elements. His quiet and definitive presence imparted a feeling of certainty among colleagues, filling in as a settling force despite the innate vulnerabilities of remote ocean investigation. Commandant Mitchell's initiative style stressed clear correspondence and a common feeling of direction, cultivating a cooperative climate where every part felt esteemed and comprehended.

Dr. Emily Chang, the geologist, carried her logical mentality and accuracy to the group. In the early arranging stages, she worked intimately with Leader Mitchell to distinguish key geographical destinations for investigation. Dr. Chang's capacity to make an interpretation of intricate geographical ideas into significant plans guaranteed that the mission's goals adjusted flawlessly with the abilities of the Submarine Stories Titan. Her job became instrumental in characterizing the geographical parts of the campaign and giving a strong groundwork to the group's logical undertakings.

Dr. Alan Rodriguez, the roboticist, confronted the underlying test of coordinating high level automated innovation into the mission. As the group wrestled with the complexities of the Titan's automated arms, Dr. Rodriguez arose as an issue solver and a scaffold among innovation and science. His cooperative methodology included close correspondence with the sea life scholars, geologists, and submariners to fit the automated arms' functionalities to the different requirements of the mission. Dr.

Rodriguez's flexibility and eagerness to repeat on plans guaranteed that the automated parts were finely tuned for the difficulties of the remote ocean.

Dr. Marcus Thompson, the sea life scholar spend significant time in bioluminescent living beings, imbued the group with a feeling of marvel and interest. His energy for the expected revelations in the sea's profundities went about as an impetus, igniting the minds of his partners. Dr. Thompson's job stretched out past logical mastery; he turned into a narrator, winding around stories of the mind boggling life frames that could look for them in the void. His capacity to convey the significance of their central goal in the more extensive setting of sea life science infused a more profound feeling of direction into the group's aggregate undertaking.

As the group dynamic developed, starting difficulties emerged in synchronizing the different ranges of abilities and procedures. The progress from hypothetical wanting to pragmatic execution uncovered the requirement for consistent coordination between disciplines. Geologists needed to pass the meaning of explicit stone arrangements on to roboticists, who, thusly, needed to adjust their innovation to meet the geologists' necessities. Sea life scientists expected to adjust their exploration objectives to the general mission goals, guaranteeing that the Titan's capacities were saddled to investigate the most encouraging districts of the sea floor.

The war room, the operational hub of the activity, filled in as the setting for the group's cooperative endeavors. Screens showing ongoing information from the Titan's fundamental plunges gave an unmistakable association with the remote ocean. As the colleagues clustered around the screens, an aggregate feeling of energy and expectation occupied the room. Nonetheless, this common energy was tempered by the acknowledgment that the excursion ahead would be full of difficulties, both known and unanticipated.

One of the early difficulties lay in improving the capacities of the Titan's automated arms. Dr. Rodriguez worked intimately with Officer Mitchell to reenact remote ocean conditions and tweak the automated arms' responsiveness. The test was not only specialized; it required a comprehension of the logical targets each discipline expected to accomplish. This iterative course of coordinated effort, change, and refinement highlighted the significance of open correspondence and shared grasping inside the group.

Dr. Chang confronted her own arrangement of difficulties in distinguishing the most encouraging land destinations for investigation. The boundlessness of the sea floor introduced an overwhelming errand, requiring a harmony between logical interest and calculated plausibility.

Through cooperative conversations with the whole group, Dr. Chang refined her land targets, guaranteeing that each site held the potential for momentous disclosures. This cycle featured the need of interdisciplinary joint effort in molding the direction of the campaign.

As the group dug further into mission arrangements, the issue of test assortment and conservation arose as a point of convergence. Dr. Chang's geographical examples, Dr. Thompson's expected natural examples, and Dr. Rodriguez's automated information all necessary careful intending to guarantee their honesty during the climb. This challenge required a cross-disciplinary comprehension of each colleague's necessities and imperatives, encouraging a culture of flexibility and shared critical thinking.

The cooperative endeavors additionally reached out to the improvement of correspondence conventions during the mission. Commandant Mitchell, with his involvement with submarine tasks, assumed a focal part in planning the progression of data between the Titan and the war room. Clear and effective correspondence became principal in addressing unexpected difficulties and adjusting to ongoing advancements during the remote ocean investigation. The group's capacity to quickly adjust to changing conditions was a demonstration of the strength of their aggregate dynamic.

As the difficulties were dealt with, the group developed more strong. Shared encounters, both in the war room and during reenacted jumps, fortified the bonds among colleagues. Dr. Hayes, perceiving the advancing group dynamic, energized normal post-op interviews where every part had the chance to share experiences and difficulties. These meetings encouraged a culture of open correspondence, where individual points of view were esteemed and coordinated into the continuous mission methodology.

The organization of the Submarine Stories Titan into the remote ocean denoted the zenith of the group's cooperative endeavors and the inception of a groundbreaking investigation. As the group noticed the constant information spilling from the Titan's cameras, mechanical arms, and logical instruments, a feeling of wonderment and expectation saturated the war room. The difficulties looked during the planning stage had fashioned a group equipped for adjusting to the obscure, embracing the erratic idea of remote ocean investigation.

The underlying phases of the mission highlighted the meaning of group elements in the progress of such complex endeavors. The mix of different disciplines, from sea life science to mechanical technology, requested individual skill as well as a common obligation to a typical reason. Dr. Hayes, as the pioneer, assumed a critical part in cultivating a climate where each colleague felt enabled to contribute their special abilities while regarding and valuing the commitments of others.

The cooperative soul of the group filled in as a main thrust, impelling the Sub Stories Titan's Maritime Investigation into unfamiliar waters. As the group faced and conquered starting difficulties, the bond among its individuals developed, making an establishment for future revelations and the getting through tradition of a group that considered investigating the secrets concealed underneath the waves. The excursion into the pit was a logical undertaking as well as a demonstration of the flexibility of human joint effort notwithstanding the unexplored world.

Chapter 2

Titan's Enigma

The Submarine Stories Titan's Maritime Investigation unfurled with a blend of expectation and fear, as the group slipped into the deep profundities, ready to disclose the riddle that lay underneath the sea's surface. The excursion into the obscure was a logical undertaking as well as an investigation into the secrets that had evaded human comprehension for quite a long time. This unfurling account, the Titan's Riddle, was bound to shape the aggregate information on the sea's secret domains.

As the Submarine Stories Titan dove further into the sea, the war room turned into a center of excited action. The group, drove by Dr. Victoria Hayes, was near the precarious edge of revelation, as time passes carrying them closer to unwinding the mysteries covered in obscurity territory of the submerged world. The war room's screens glimmered with pictures of the sea depths, uncovering a scene that swayed between distinct devastation and amazing biodiversity.

Authority James Mitchell, at the controls of the Titan, ably explored through the complex submerged territory. The strain escalated with each meter of drop, reflecting the uplifted fervor inside the war room. The Titan's mechanical arms, under the order of Dr. Alan Rodriguez, were ready for activity, prepared to gather tests and record the concealed marvels that looked for them in the profundities.

Dr. Emily Chang, the geologist, firmly noticed the unfurling geographical elements on the sea floor. The Titan's cameras caught entrancing pictures of submerged developments, giving a visual embroidery that indicated the World's geographical history. Dr. Chang's skill came to the very front as she distinguished expected destinations for test assortment, her land instinct directing the group to areas of logical importance.

Dr. Marcus Thompson, the sea life scientist with a specialization in bioluminescent living beings, was enamored by the play of light and shadows in the remote ocean. As the Titan's lights enlightened the environmental factors, Dr. Thompson wondered about the one of a kind variations of life in this outrageous climate. The bioluminescent showcases, caught by the Titan's cameras, portrayed a world that existed in unending murkiness.

The underlying snapshots of the Titan's plummet were set apart by a feeling of worship and miracle. The group, as one, looked as the sea uncovered its insider facts. Dr. Hayes, with a blend of fervor and thought, verbalized the meaning existing apart from everything else. The Titan's Mystery was not just a mission for information; it was an excursion into the core of the Earth, an investigation that looked to overcome any barrier between what was known and what stayed unseen.

As the Titan arrived at its designated profundity, the group's center moved to the careful execution of the mission's logical goals. Dr. Chang distinguished a promising geographical development, and the mechanical arms, under Dr. Rodriguez's order, were conveyed with accuracy. Tests of rocks and dregs were gathered, each piece holding the possibility to open the mysteries of the World's old past.

At the same time, Dr. Thompson coordinated the Titan's cameras toward areas of organic interest. The bioluminescent life forms, adjusted to get by in the outrageous states of the remote ocean, stunned the group with their powerful gleam. The Titan's cameras caught the complicated dance of life in the obscurity, giving an uncommon look into a domain that remained generally distant to human perception.

The coordinated effort between colleagues turned out to be more articulated as they deciphered the continuous information gushing from the Titan. Dr. Chang's land discoveries informed Dr. How Thompson might interpret the natural circumstances that formed marine life. Dr. Rodriguez, thus, changed the mechanical arms' developments in light of the powerful criticism from both the geographical and natural groups. The union of skill was a demonstration of the strength of the interdisciplinary methodology embraced by the Sub Stories Titan's Maritime Investigation.

Notwithstanding, in the midst of the remarkable disclosures, challenges arose. The Titan's Puzzler was not without its deterrents, and the group confronted startling obstacles that tried their versatility and strength.

As the Titan explored through tight sections and experienced unfamiliar submerged highlights, the requirement for speedy reasoning and cooperative critical thinking became clear.

One such test emerged when the Titan's mechanical arm experienced opposition while endeavoring to gather a land test. The group, confronted with the surprising hindrance, assembled quickly to survey what is happening. Dr. Rodriguez, in a joint effort with Commandant Mitchell, changed the submarine's situation, while Dr. Chang gave experiences into the idea of the substrate. The planned exertion brought about the effective assortment of the example, featuring the group's capacity to conquer impediments continuously.

The Titan's Mystery kept on unfurling, uncovering the miracles of the remote ocean as well as the versatility of the human soul notwithstanding the unexplored world. The group, limited by a common feeling of direction, pushed forward, anxious to test further into the secrets that encompassed them. Dr. Hayes, as the directing power, underlined the significance of embracing vulnerability and survey difficulties as any open doors for disclosure.

As the Titan proceeded with its investigation, the group experienced a district of the sea depths set apart by curiously elevated degrees of topographical action. Dr. Chang, her land impulses increased, perceived the meaning of this disclosure. The Titan's cameras caught volcanic vents, delivering tufts of hot, mineral-rich liquids into the sea. The ramifications of this finding were significant, offering bits of knowledge into the World's geothermal cycles and the potential for novel biological systems to flourish in these outrageous circumstances.

The organic group, drove by Dr. Thompson, enthusiastically examined the regions encompassing the volcanic vents. The Titan's cameras uncovered an astonishing cluster of living things, adjusted to flourish in the cruel climate made by the geothermal action. Minute creatures, already obscure to science, prospered in the supplement rich waters encompassing the vents. The disclosure ignited a recharged feeling of energy and interest inside the group, highlighting the significance of wandering into the obscure to uncover stowed away biological specialties.

In the midst of the logical disclosures, the Titan's Puzzler additionally provoked philosophical reflections on mankind's relationship with the sea. Dr. Hayes, in a snapshot of examination, discussed the interconnectedness of all life on The planet and the obligation people bore as stewards of the seas. The Titan's excursion, she underscored, was a logical undertaking as well as a source of inspiration to safeguard and protect these fragile environments.

As the Sub Stories Titan proceeded with its investigation, the group experienced a peculiarity that additional one more layer to the mystery. Unidentified submerged structures, looking like perplexing arrangements of stone, arose out of the ocean bottom.

The Titan's cameras caught pictures of these perplexing designs, inciting hypothesis and interest among the colleagues. Dr. Chang, drawing on her geographical mastery, placed speculations about the beginning of these developments, bringing up issues that would fuel future exploration tries.

The unforeseen disclosures and difficulties looked by the group highlighted the powerful idea of remote ocean investigation. The Titan's Riddle was not a straight movement of logical request but rather a progression of exciting bends in the road that requested ceaseless variation and learning. The strength of the group, their capacity to explore vulnerabilities, and the soul of cooperative investigation characterized the campaign's prosperity.

As the Titan rose from the profundities, the group thought about the significant effect of their excursion. The information gathered, the examples got, and the pictures caught would add to a more profound comprehension of the sea's secrets. Dr. Hayes, tending to the group in a post-op interview meeting, offered thanks for their aggregate endeavors and stressed the significance of making an interpretation of their discoveries into noteworthy information to help people in the future.

The Titan's Mystery, while opening a portion of the privileged insights concealed underneath the waves, likewise featured the tremendousness of the sea's obscure domains. The endeavor was a demonstration of the dauntless human soul, driven by a voracious interest to investigate the strange and defy the secrets that keep on escaping our comprehension. The Submarine Stories Titan's Maritime Investigation, directed by the group's skill and cooperative soul, made a permanent imprint on the chronicles of marine investigation and prepared for future excursions into the cryptic profundities of the World's last outskirts.

2.1 Delve into the scientific mysteries surrounding Titan's ocean.

The logical secrets encompassing Titan's sea, a domain hidden in the perplexing environment of Saturn's biggest moon, have enraptured the minds of researchers and specialists. The Submarine Stories Titan's Maritime Investigation left on a pivotal mission to unwind these secrets, trying to understand the intricacies of an extraterrestrial sea and attract equals to the basic cycles forming Earth's own oceanic surroundings.

Titan's sea, hid underneath a thick climate of nitrogen and methane, presents a novel arrangement of difficulties and open doors for logical request. Dr. Victoria Hayes, the visionary head of the undertaking, outlined the investigation inside the setting of astrobiology - the investigation of the potential for life past Earth. The secrets of Titan's sea reached out past its fluid hydrocarbon creation, coaxing the group to dive into the key structure blocks of life and the circumstances that could cultivate its presence.

One of the essential logical goals of the Titan investigation was to grasp the piece and properties of the fluid in Titan's oceans. Dissimilar to Earth's water-based seas, Titan's oceans are made out of hydrocarbons, essentially ethane and methane. The Titanian climate, portrayed by outrageous cold and ethereal scenes, suggested conversation starters about the elements of these hydrocarbon oceans. How could they act under Titan's cold circumstances, and what synthetic cycles administered their communications with the moon's surface?

Dr. Emily Chang, the geologist in the group, assumed a significant part in deciphering the topographical highlights encompassing Titan's sea. The Titanian scene, set apart by immense rises and ethereal lakes, indicated dynamic cycles molding the moon's surface. The relationship between's geographical developments and the sythesis of Titan's oceans gave important bits of knowledge into the moon's land history. Dr. Chang's land investigations intended to uncover the powers chiseling Titan's surface and the interconnectedness of its geographical and hydrocarbon frameworks.

As the Submarine Stories Titan plunged into Titan's sea, the group experienced startling varieties in the piece and temperature of the fluid hydrocarbons. These varieties ignited logical interest, inciting Dr. Chang to conjecture about the expected presence of submerged geothermal highlights or hydrocarbon vents. The exchange between land processes and the structure of Titan's sea turned into a point of convergence of examination, welcoming correlations with Earth's aqueous frameworks and their job in encouraging different environments.

Dr. Alan Rodriguez, the roboticist supervising the Titan's mechanical arms, assumed an essential part in the investigation of Titan's sea floor. The mechanical arms, outfitted with cutting edge sensors and inspecting apparatuses, permitted the group to gather information and tests from the moon's seabed. The puzzle of Titan's sea reached out past its surface, provoking inquiries regarding the idea of its seabed, the possible presence of subsurface repositories, and the geographical elements that molded its submerged scene.

As the Titan's automated arms contacted gather tests from the sea depths, the group was met with surprising opposition. The seabed, made out of a blend of frosty residue and hydrocarbon-rich stores, introduced difficulties in example assortment. Dr. Rodriguez, drawing on his aptitude, adjusted the automated arms' methodologies, displaying the group's capacity to conquer specialized difficulties chasing after logical disclosure. The gathered examples held the commitment of opening pieces of information about Titan's topographical history and the cycles forming its maritime climate.

Dr. Marcus Thompson, the sea life scientist having some expertise in bioluminescent living beings, coordinated the Titan's cameras toward areas of possible natural interest. The presence of life in Titan's sea, while speculative, stayed an enticing possibility.

That's what the group estimated if life somehow happened to exist, it could appear in structures adjusted to the special science and states of Titan's oceans. The Titanian environment, if without a doubt possessed, might grandstand novel transformations and biochemical pathways unmistakable from those on The planet.

The Titan's Puzzler reached out to the chance of prebiotic science in Titan's sea - the complicated natural particles that could act as the structure blocks forever. The wealth of natural mixtures in Titan's air, joined with the presence of fluid hydrocarbons on its surface, established a climate helpful for the combination of mind boggling particles. Dr. Thompson's interest with the potential for bioluminescent organic entities in Titan's sea reflected the group's more extensive interest about the possibility of extraordinary living things flourishing in this extraterrestrial ocean.

While the Sub Stories Titan's Maritime Investigation basically centered around logical request, the mission additionally embraced the more extensive ramifications for astrobiology and our comprehension of life past Earth. Dr. Hayes, in tending to the group and the worldwide crowd following the mission, underlined the meaning of Titan's sea as a window into the possible variety of livable conditions in our planetary group and then some. The secrets encompassing Titan's sea reached out past the prompt logical perceptions, moving mankind to examine the more extensive ramifications for the quest for extraterrestrial life.

The investigation of Titan's sea additionally brought up issues about the moon's environment and weather conditions. Titan, with its thick environment and occasional cycles, encounters precipitation as fluid methane and ethane downpour. The effect of these hydrocarbon rainfalls on the sythesis and elements of Titan's sea turned into a subject of logical examination. Dr. Hayes proposed that the recurrent convergence of hydrocarbons could add to the recharging and rearrangement of substances inside the sea, affecting its synthetic piece and the potential for dynamic cycles.

As the Sub Stories Titan proceeded with its investigation, the group experienced one of a kind peculiarities inside the moon's sea. The Titanian oceans, encompassed by ethereal scenes and interspersed by geographical arrangements, uncovered the complexities of a climate formed by the interaction of science, topography, and environment. The Titan's Mystery unfurled as an embroidery of logical disclosures, provoking the group to refine how they might interpret extraterrestrial seas and their possible ramifications for the quest for life past Earth.

The puzzler of Titan's sea reached out to the more extensive setting of planetary science, provoking specialists to draw matches between the cycles forming Titan and those administering Earth's seas.

The Titanian framework, with its intricate interchange of topographical, air, and hydrocarbon processes, filled in as an extraordinary research center for near planetology. Dr. Chang, drawing on her land mastery, featured the potential for cross-disciplinary bits of knowledge that could educate our comprehension regarding planetary development and the elements affecting livability.

The Sub Stories Titan's Maritime Investigation, in its mission to unwind the secrets encompassing Titan's sea, likewise added to our more extensive comprehension of the tenability of frosty moons inside our nearby planet group. The potential for subsurface seas on moons like Europa and Enceladus, holding onto conditions helpful for life, attracted equals to the investigation of Titan's sea. Dr. Hayes underscored the interconnectedness of logical request, imagining a future where examples gained from Titan could illuminate the methodologies for investigating other divine bodies.

As the mission advanced, the group wrestled with the puzzle of Titan's sea's expected livability. While the super cold and hydrocarbon organization acted difficulties for life like we know it, the versatile idea of living things on Earth provoked hypothesis about the chance of colorful biochemistries flourishing in Titan's oceans. Dr. Thompson, in a joint effort with astrobiologists in the group, investigated the hypothetical systems for life's expected transformation to Titan's extraordinary ecological circumstances, growing the skylines of astrobiological research.

The Titan's Conundrum, past its logical ramifications, resounded with the more extensive human undertaking to investigate the unexplored world. The investigation of Titan's sea turned into a demonstration of the human soul's voracious interest and the drive to grow the limits of information. Dr. Hayes, thinking about the mission's accomplishments, discussed the aggregate human excursion into the universe and the meaning of each step taken in the investigation of our heavenly neighbors.

As the Sub Stories Titan's Maritime Investigation finished up its main goal and the Titan's Riddle turned out to be essential for the logical story, the group got back with a stash of information, tests, and experiences. The mission's inheritance reached out past the prompt logical disclosures, impacting future investigation attempts and forming the direction of planetary science. Titan's sea, when a riddle hidden in the secrets of the universe, yielded its mysteries to the curious look of human investigation, denoting a section in the continuous adventure of mankind's mission to grasp the complexities of the universe.

2.2 Unravel the known and unknown aspects of Titan's unique environment.

Titan, Saturn's biggest moon, has long remained as a divine mystery, special climate covered in secrets coax researchers to disentangle the intricacies of this far off world.

The Submarine Stories Titan's Maritime Investigation wandered into the core of Titan's secrets, meaning to investigate both the known and obscure parts of its solitary climate. As the mission dove into unknown domains, it defied a bunch of inquiries regarding Titan's environment, surface highlights, and the mysterious subsurface sea that lay underneath its bone chilling outside.

Known for its thick environment, Titan flaunts a complicated science that separates it from other heavenly bodies in our nearby planet group. Made fundamentally out of nitrogen, with hints of methane and ethane, Titan's climate establishes a powerful climate. Dr. Victoria Hayes, the undertaking's chief, underscored the meaning of Titan's climate as a central participant in molding the moon's exceptional qualities. The Submarine Stories Titan's Maritime Investigation looked to comprehend the interaction between Titan's climatic piece and the unique cycles happening on its surface and subsurface.

The investigation started with an emphasis on Titan's surface, described by huge ridges and lakes. These lakes, nonetheless, were not made out of water but instead of fluid methane and ethane. Dr. Emily Chang, the geologist in the group, assumed a pivotal part in unraveling the topographical elements that molded Titan's scene. The known parts of Titan's surface incorporate sweeping oceans and pools of hydrocarbons, where fluid methane and ethane go through unique cycles like Earth's water cycle, but at a lot colder temperature.

As the Submarine Stories Titan plunged through Titan's climate, the known elements of the moon's surface came into more keen concentration. The huge hydrocarbon lakes, reflecting Earth's waterways, turned into a dazzling subject of logical examination. Dr. Chang's geographical investigations expected to disentangle the land history engraved on Titan's surface. The ridges, suggestive of those tracked down in Earth's deserts, alluded to wind-driven processes that formed the moon's sweeping fields.

The Titanian scene, with its ethereal lakes and hills, introduced a dreamlike juxtaposition of natural and outsider highlights. The known parts of Titan's surface, impacted by hydrocarbon processes, brought up issues about the unique powers molding the moon's geology. Dr. Chang hypothesized that Titan's land development could include a mix of structural cycles, cryovolcanism, and erosional powers, giving a rich embroidery to logical examination.

Be that as it may, the known highlights of Titan's surface just start to expose the moon's secrets. The group directed their concentration toward the obscure parts of Titan's current circumstance, especially its subsurface sea. The presence of a subsurface sea had for some time been hypothesized, in light of perceptions of Titan's gravitational collaborations with Saturn and the moon's surface elements. The Submarine Stories Titan's Maritime Investigation denoted a memorable undertaking to test the obscure profundities and open the insider facts disguised underneath Titan's frigid outside.

Dr. Alan Rodriguez, the roboticist managing the mission's mechanical arms, assumed a significant part in the investigation of Titan's subsurface sea. The obscure parts of this sea held the commitment of momentous revelations, possibly offering experiences into the moon's tenability and the more extensive ramifications for the quest for life past Earth. The automated arms, furnished with cutting edge sensors and testing apparatuses, were ready to gather information and tests from the sea depths, revealing insight into the strange domain concealed underneath the ice.

As the Submarine Stories Titan dropped into Titan's sea, the obscure parts of the subsurface climate turned into the point of convergence of logical expectation. The group wrestled with inquiries concerning the sea's profundity, its organization, and the potential for interesting topographical elements on the sea depths. Dr. Chang, with her land ability, estimated about the idea of the seabed and the interconnectedness between Titan's surface and subsurface cycles.

The known and obscure parts of Titan's current circumstance were complicatedly associated, provoking the group to think about the more extensive setting of the moon's geographical and climatic collaborations. The presence of a subsurface sea, whenever affirmed, would have significant ramifications for Titan's livability and the potential for prebiotic science. Dr. Marcus Thompson, the sea life researcher spend significant time in bioluminescent organic entities, examined the chance of life in Titan's sea and the transformation of novel life structures to its outrageous circumstances.

The Submarine Stories Titan's Maritime Investigation, as it wandered into Titan's sea, experienced surprising varieties in the structure and temperature of the fluid hydrocarbons. The obscure parts of the sea's elements became clear, provoking the group to adjust their methodology continuously. Dr. Rodriguez, at the controls of the Titan's automated arms, displayed the group's capacity to defeat difficulties and make on-the-fly changes in accordance with the mission's logical targets.

As the automated arms contacted gather tests from the sea depths, the group wrestled with the obscure parts of Titan's geographical elements. The subsurface sea, while holding the offer of uncovering too much's land history, likewise introduced difficulties in example assortment. Dr. Chang, drawing on her geographical instinct, proposed about the potential for submerged geothermal elements or hydrocarbon vents, adding layers to the obscure parts of Titan's maritime climate.

Dr. Thompson, with an emphasis on the potential for bioluminescent organic entities in Titan's sea, coordinated the Titan's cameras toward areas of natural interest. The obscure parts of life in Titan's sea started logical interest and hypothesis about the expected variations of life structures to the novel science and states of the moon's subsurface climate.

The transaction between the known and obscure parts of Titan's sea highlighted the interdisciplinary idea of the mission and the powerful coordinated effort among colleagues.

The investigation of Titan's sea provoked reflections on the more extensive ramifications for how we might interpret the tenability of cold moons in our nearby planet group and then some. The known and obscure parts of Titan's current circumstance, as uncovered by the Submarine Stories Titan's Maritime Investigation, added to the continuous story of astrobiology - the quest for life past Earth. Dr. Hayes, in tending to the group and the worldwide crowd following the mission, highlighted the significance of Titan as a likely research center for concentrating on the circumstances that could cultivate life in different planetary conditions.

As the Sub Stories Titan's Maritime Investigation proceeded with its main goal, the group experienced extraordinary peculiarities inside the moon's sea. The known and obscure parts of Titan's current circumstance became entwined in a story that unfurled with each jump into the maritime profundities. The Titanian oceans, encompassed by ethereal scenes and accentuated by topographical arrangements, uncovered the complexities of a climate molded by the interchange of science, topography, and environment.

The investigation of Titan's sea, with its known and obscure aspects, reached out past logical request. It turned into a demonstration of the human soul's unquenchable interest and the drive to investigate the unexplored world. The group, limited by a common feeling of direction, stood up to the secrets of Titan's current circumstance with a mix of logical thoroughness and creative marvel. Dr. Hayes, thinking about the mission's accomplishments, discussed the aggregate human excursion into the universe and the meaning of each step taken in the investigation of our heavenly neighbors.

The known and obscure parts of Titan's remarkable climate, as disentangled by the Submarine Stories Titan's Maritime Investigation, denoted a critical second in our mission to fathom the variety of universes inside our nearby planet group. Titan, when a far off riddle, yielded its privileged insights to the curious look of human investigation, welcoming us to ponder the more extensive ramifications for the quest forever and the powerful cycles molding the universe. The excursion into Titan's secrets, with its known and obscure domains, extended the boondocks of human information and coaxed future voyagers to proceed with the tradition of disclosure in the divine scope.

2.3 The team faces skepticism and challenges from the scientific community.

The Sub Stories Titan's Maritime Investigation, while a great undertaking, confronted a considerable test past the ranges of Titan's environment — the suspicion and difficulties from mainstream researchers.

As insight about the mission spread, questions emerged inside established researchers about the plausibility of investigating Titan's sea and the expected profits from such an intricate and exorbitant endeavor. Dr. Victoria Hayes, the head of the undertaking, wound up exploring the profundities of Titan's moon as well as the wariness and investigates reverberating inside the logical domain.

The doubt principally originated from the dauntlessness of the mission's objectives — to send a submarine into the subsurface expanse of a far off moon. The extraordinary idea of the mission ignited banters about asset assignment, the prioritization of logical undertakings, and the innate dangers related with wandering into strange domains. Some doubted whether the expected revelations in Titan's sea legitimized the significant speculation and whether elective missions could yield more quick and unmistakable outcomes.

Dr. Hayes, mindful of the distrust, embraced the obligation of upholding for the logical value of the Submarine Stories Titan's Maritime Investigation. In light of evaluates, she underlined the extraordinary logical inquiries the mission meant to address. The subsurface expanse of Titan, accepted to be wealthy in hydrocarbons and possibly holding onto one of a kind types of life, introduced an unmatched chance to extend how we might interpret extraterrestrial conditions and the potential for tenability past Earth.

The provokes reached out past wariness to the reasonable items of executing such a perplexing mission. Dr. Alan Rodriguez, directing the automated arms indispensable to the investigation, confronted distrust about the attainability of gathering significant information from Titan's sea floor. Pundits scrutinized the versatility of automated innovation to the outrageous states of the moon's subsurface climate, communicating worries about the accuracy and unwavering quality of the mechanical arms neglected and hydrocarbon-rich environmental elements.

In light of these worries, Dr. Rodriguez and his group set out on thorough testing and recreation processes. They repeated the states of Titan's sea floor, calibrating the mechanical arms' functionalities to guarantee ideal execution. These endeavors, while tedious, were vital in tending to the doubt encompassing the mission's mechanical viewpoints. The group intended to exhibit that, notwithstanding the difficulties, the Submarine Stories Titan's Maritime Investigation was prepared to beat the cruel circumstances and convey significant logical bits of knowledge.

Dr. Emily Chang, the geologist contributing her mastery to the mission, confronted incredulity about the expected land meaning of Titan's sea floor. A few researchers addressed whether the frosty moon's seabed held land developments of interest, taking into account the known hydrocarbon lakes on its surface. Dr. Chang, unfazed, contended that the potential for one of a kind geographical elements in the subsurface sea was a basic part of Titan's secrets.

To address these worries, Dr. Chang took part in cooperative conversations with associates spend significant time in planetary geography. She introduced speculations about the interaction between the moon's surface and subsurface cycles, proposing that the sea floor could uncover fundamental pieces of information about Titan's land development. The objective was to show that the mission's logical targets stretched out past the surface and into the profundities of Titan's baffling sea.

Dr. Marcus Thompson, the sea life researcher, confronted wariness about the potential for life in Titan's sea. The super cool, the piece of the fluid hydrocarbons, and the shortfall of fluid water on the moon's surface drove some to scrutinize the achievability of finding living things adjusted to such unforgiving circumstances. Dr. Thompson, attracting on his ability extremophiles on The planet, contended that life might actually adjust to Titan's novel climate.

The distrust encompassing the potential for life in Titan's sea provoked Dr. Thompson to team up with astrobiologists and exobiologists inside mainstream researchers. Together, they dug into hypothetical structures for life in eccentric conditions, investigating the restrictions of versatility and the potential for outlandish biochemistries. The objective was to overcome any barrier among distrust and logical creative mind, displaying that the Sub Stories Titan's Maritime Investigation was not just a mission of interest but rather a journey to resolve significant inquiries regarding the potential for life past Earth.

Regardless of these endeavors, the suspicion inside established researchers persevered, for certain scientists pushing for elective missions with additional quick applications or more clear pathways to notable disclosures. The difficulties looked by the group reached out past the specialized parts of the mission to the requirement for successful correspondence and effort. Dr. Hayes perceived the significance of straightforwardly tending to worries inside established researchers and the more extensive public to earn support for the mission's aggressive objectives.

In light of the wariness, the group coordinated discussions and gatherings to introduce their examination discoveries, systems, and the logical reasoning behind the Submarine Stories Titan's Maritime Investigation. These gatherings gave a stage to open exchange, empowering the group to draw in with individual researchers, address concerns, and refine their methodology in view of helpful criticism. Dr. Hayes, in her job as the campaign's chief, turned into a vocal promoter for the mission, underscoring the potential for outlook changing disclosures and the basic of pushing the limits of logical investigation.

The group additionally perceived the significance of including the more extensive public in their logical excursion. Dr. Alan Rodriguez, utilizing his skill in mechanical innovation, started instructive projects that permitted understudies and lovers to collaborate with mimicked mechanical arms, encouraging a feeling of association with the mission's targets.

Dr. Marcus Thompson, with his experience in sea life science, participated out in the open talks and effort projects to convey the fervor of investigating Titan's sea and the potential for finding exceptional living things.

The Sub Stories Titan's Maritime Investigation turned out to be in excess of a logical mission — it changed into a story of human desire, interest, and the quest for information. Dr. Hayes, in meetings and public locations, talked enthusiastically about the innate benefit of pushing the limits of investigation, even notwithstanding suspicion. She accentuated that logical undertakings, especially those investigating the obscure, frequently confronted suspicion at first however could possibly reclassify how we might interpret the universe.

The group's excursion into Titan's mysterious sea, regardless of the distrust and difficulties, turned into a demonstration of the strength of logical investigation. The Submarine Stories Titan's Maritime Investigation, as it explored the profundities of Titan's moon and the intricacies of logical examination, highlighted the iterative idea of revelation. Dr. Emily Chang, considering the difficulties looked by the group, underscored the significance of embracing incredulity as a main thrust for refining techniques and reinforcing the logical groundwork of the mission.

As the Submarine Stories Titan's Maritime Investigation advanced, the distrust inside mainstream researchers steadily developed into a blend of careful confidence and certifiable interest. The group's obligation to straightforwardness, joint effort, and public commitment assumed a significant part in collecting support for their main goal. The discussions and meetings that were once fields for wariness changed into stages for shared energy and expectation as the group disclosed primer discoveries and experiences from Titan's sea.

The difficulties looked by the group, both inside and outside mainstream researchers, became necessary to the mission's story. The Sub Stories Titan's Maritime Investigation, once met with incredulity, presently remained as an image of human inventiveness and the quest for information against the background of the grandiose unexplored world. The mission's unfurling story, with its turns, turns, and snapshots of win, repeated the more extensive human undertaking to investigate and figure out the secrets that lie past our earthbound limits.

In the last phases of the mission, as the Submarine Stories Titan's Maritime Investigation approached its decision, the group thought about the extraordinary excursion they had attempted. The wariness that at first encompassed the mission had, in numerous ways, energized the group's assurance to defeat difficulties and exhibit the logical benefit of investigating Titan's sea. Dr. Hayes, tending to mainstream researchers in a finishing up conference, recognized the studies and distrust as vital parts of the logical cycle.

The Sub Stories Titan's Maritime Investigation, completely, turned into a contextual analysis in determination, coordinated effort, and the unyielding soul of investigation. The group, once met with incredulity, had effectively explored the intricacies of an extraordinary mission, conveying important bits of knowledge into the secrets of Titan's one of a kind climate. Mainstream researchers, at first separated, presently stood joined in praising the achievements of a mission that really considered wandering where none had gone previously.

As the Sub Stories Titan's Maritime Investigation finished up, the tradition of the mission stretched out past the logical disclosures. It turned into a guide of motivation for people in the future of researchers, designers, and wayfarers. The suspicion that once tested the mission's legitimacy currently filled in as a demonstration of the innate difficulties of investigating the grandiose unexplored world. The Submarine Stories

Titan's Maritime Investigation, with its story of wariness, strength, and win, joined the records of human investigation, making a permanent imprint on the continuous journey to disentangle the secrets of the universe.

Chapter 3

The Submersible: Titan Voyager

The Sub: Titan Explorer, an aggressive mission set in the vast background of Saturn's biggest moon, set out on an excursion that rose above the limits of conventional space investigation. Driven by Dr. Victoria Hayes, a visionary researcher enthusiastically for unwinding the secrets of the planetary group, the mission meant to dig into the profundities of Titan's perplexing sea, a domain clouded underneath layers of frigid interest.

The excursion of the Titan Explorer started with careful preparation and planning. The group, contained researchers, specialists, and travelers from different fields, assembled at the mission control focus, an operational hub throbbing with expectation. Dr. Hayes, the directing power behind the endeavor, tended to the group with a blend of energy and assurance, highlighting the meaning of investigating Titan's sea — a space that vowed to open privileged insights about the moon's geographical history, expected tenability, and the more extensive secrets of the universe.

Commandant James Mitchell, an accomplished space explorer in charge of the Titan Explorer, handily moved the submarine through the multifaceted dance of Saturn's rings. The excursion through space, with the ringed goliath as a divine sidekick, set up for the impending plunge into Titan's climate.

The group observed each part of the mission, from route to air section, with an accuracy that mirrored the zenith of long periods of logical mastery and mechanical development.

As the Titan Explorer dropped through Titan's thick environment, the group experienced moves special to this far off moon. The cold murkiness that hidden Titan's surface introduced a navigational riddle, requiring exact changes in accordance with guarantee a protected drop. Dr. Alan Rodriguez, the roboticist administering the mission's mechanical parts, worked couple with Authority Mitchell to explore through the barometrical intricacies. The mechanical arms, furnished with cutting edge sensors and examining apparatuses, were ready for activity, prepared to gather information and tests from Titan's surface.

The Titan Explorer, furnished with cutting edge instruments, infiltrated the cloudiness and uncovered the moon's surface — a scene set apart by huge rises and ethereal lakes. The known highlights of Titan's surface, including pools of fluid methane and ethane, enraptured the group as they wondered about the extraordinary excellence unfurling on their screens. Dr. Emily Chang, the geologist, coordinated the consideration of the Titan Explorer toward possible geographical focal points, making way for the mission's investigation of Titan's surface.

The Titan Explorer's drop kept, changing from the cold surface to the frosty profundities of Titan's sea. The group, eagerly, observed the submarine's advancement as it entered the subsurface climate. Dr. Marcus Thompson, the sea life scholar, enthusiastically expected the potential for finding life in Titan's sea, a possibility that lighted logical interest and started conversations about the flexibility of life structures in outrageous extraterrestrial conditions.

The investigation of Titan's sea was a mission full of vulnerabilities and energy. The Submarine: Titan Explorer, with its automated arms expanded, started the methodical assortment of tests from the sea floor. Dr. Rodriguez, arranging the mechanical moves, experienced startling varieties in the sythesis and temperature of the fluid hydrocarbons, alluding to the unique idea of Titan's subsurface climate.

As the Titan Explorer explored the sea's profundities, the group confronted difficulties that tried their creativity and flexibility. Dr. Hayes, with a quiet purpose, directed the group through unexpected deterrents, stressing the significance of adaptability and cooperation. The mission, set apart by the two victories and difficulties, unfurled as a demonstration of the human soul's strength even with the unexplored world.

Dr. Chang, examining the land highlights on the sea depths, recognized developments that alluded to Titan's geographical history. The collaboration between the cold covering and the fluid hydrocarbons underneath divulged a story of dynamic cycles forming the moon's subsurface climate. The Titan Explorer, through its automated arms, gathered examples that held the possibility to disentangle the secrets hid underneath the maritime profundities.

Dr. Thompson, coordinating the Titan Explorer's cameras toward likely organic areas of interest, wondered about the possibility of finding life in Titan's sea. The group guessed about the transformations living things could have gone through to flourish in this outrageous climate. The Titan Explorer's cameras caught pictures of the obscure, igniting conversations inside the group and across mainstream researchers about the potential for finding extraordinary biochemistries and novel types of life.

The Submarine: Titan Explorer confronted not just the difficulties of investigating an extraterrestrial sea yet additionally the examination of mainstream researchers. The daringness of the mission started banters about asset assignment, the likely profits from speculation, and the more extensive ramifications for the eventual fate of room investigation. Dr. Hayes, mindful of the suspicion, participated in discoursed with individual researchers, introducing the mission as a spearheading try that pushed the limits of investigation and added to humankind's developing comprehension of the universe.

The difficulties looked by the Titan Explorer stretched out to the specialized complexities of working a sub in an outsider climate. Dr. Rodriguez, addressing worries about the versatility of mechanical innovation to Titan's sea floor, displayed the progress of the automated arms in gathering tests and exploring the perplexing geography. The innovative accomplishments of the mission, while not safe to doubt, showed the plausibility of investigating Titan's subsurface sea with cutting edge advanced mechanics.

Dr. Thompson, tending to doubt about the potential for life in Titan's sea, underlined the more extensive ramifications for astrobiology and the quest for extraterrestrial life. The disclosures made by the Titan Explorer, even without any authoritative confirmation of life, added to the developing assortment of information about the circumstances that could cultivate life past Earth. The group's obligation to straightforwardness, combined with the logical thoroughness applied to the mission, assumed a vital part in reshaping discernments inside mainstream researchers.

As the Sub: Titan Explorer proceeded with its investigation, the group experienced startling peculiarities that additional layers to the mission's story. Unidentified designs on the sea depths, atypical varieties in temperature, and perplexing geographical arrangements provoked the group to reevaluate how they might interpret Titan's subsurface climate. Dr. Chang, drawing on her topographical mastery, drove the group in unraveling the ramifications of these revelations, perceiving that Titan's secrets stretched out past the expected.

The unforeseen difficulties and revelations just heightened the logical talk encompassing the Submarine: Titan Explorer. Established researchers, when incredulous, wound up brought into the unfurling account of the mission. The group's commitment to thorough logical request, combined with their capacity to adjust to unexpected conditions, accumulated regard and backing from their companions.

The Submarine: Titan Explorer, in its central goal to investigate the known and obscure parts of Titan's novel climate, turned into an image of human creativity and assurance. Dr. Hayes, thinking about the excursion, discussed the mission's heritage reaching out past the prompt logical revelations. The Titan Explorer, through its investigation of Titan's sea, roused another age of researchers and wayfarers to push the limits of information and embrace the difficulties of the inestimable unexplored world.

As the mission moved toward its decision, the group assembled for a post-op interview, considering the extraordinary excursion into Titan's sea. The Submarine: Titan Explorer, once met with wariness, had effectively explored the intricacies of an extraordinary mission, making a permanent imprint on the continuous adventure of human investigation. The disclosures made, the difficulties survive, and the examples learned turned out to be essential for the logical story, adding to mankind's aggregate comprehension of the secrets that overrun our nearby planet group.

The tradition of the Submarine: Titan Explorer, with its known and obscure disclosures, resounded through the halls of logical establishments and reverberated with the more extensive public. Dr. Hayes, tending to the worldwide crowd in a finishing up proclamation, stressed the significance of interest driven investigation in extending the boondocks of human information. The Titan Explorer, in its mission to grasp Titan's sea, turned into a reference point of motivation, welcoming mankind to focus on the stars and dream of the secrets ready to be revealed in the grandiose expanse of potential outcomes.

3.1 Introduce the cutting-edge submersible, Titan Voyager.

The Titan Explorer, a state of the art submarine of unrivaled plan and refinement, addresses an essential headway in space investigation innovation. Imagined as a component of the Sub Stories Titan's Maritime Investigation mission, the Titan Explorer was designed to explore the extraterrestrial profundities of Titan, Saturn's biggest moon, and dive into its cryptic subsurface sea. Driven by the visionary researcher Dr. Victoria Hayes, the mission meant to unwind the secrets concealed underneath the cold outside of Titan and investigate the potential for life in its fluid hydrocarbon oceans.

The conceptualization of the Titan Explorer rose up out of the requirement for a particular vehicle fit for enduring the outrageous circumstances special to Titan. With its thick environment and cold surface, Titan presented difficulties unmistakable from those experienced in past space investigation missions. Dr. Hayes, perceiving the requirement for development, led a cooperative exertion that united researchers, specialists, and mechanical technology specialists to plan a submarine custom-made to the intricacies of Titan's current circumstance.

At the core of the Titan Explorer's plan is its flexibility to both surface and subsurface investigation. The sub flaunts a double usefulness that permits it to explore the frozen fields of Titan's surface and dive into the profundities of its subsurface sea. This flexibility positions the Titan Explorer as a progressive device for exhaustive investigation, empowering researchers to concentrate on the moon's geography, environment, and expected livability in remarkable detail.

The outside of the Titan Explorer is a wonder of designing, developed from cutting edge materials fit for enduring the super cold and tension circumstances pervasive on Titan. The submarine's external shell is outfitted with warm protection to safeguard it from the chilling temperatures, while its hearty construction guarantees sturdiness in the unforgiving climate. The plan likewise consolidates a set-up of sensors and instruments to catch many information, including temperature, tension, and creation of Titan's environment and sea.

One of the champion highlights of the Titan Explorer is its high level automated arms, under the direction of Dr. Alan Rodriguez, the mission's roboticist. These mechanical extremities, furnished with accuracy devices and sensors, assume a urgent part in example assortment and examination. The arms are able to do gently moving through Titan's assorted landscapes, from frosty rises on a superficial level to possible geographical developments on the sea floor. Dr. Rodriguez's mastery guarantees that the mechanical arms are versatile as well as receptive to the powerful difficulties experienced during the mission.

Exploring Titan's thick air requires progressed drive frameworks, and the Titan Explorer consolidates state of the art impetus innovation. Planned by a group of aeronautics designers under the initiative of Dr. Hayden Carter, the impetus framework empowers the sub to enter Titan's environment with accuracy and explore its surface and subsurface landscapes really. The drive framework's proficiency is significant for the outcome of the mission, permitting the Titan Explorer to execute complex moves and gather important information.

The Titan Explorer's logical payload, arranged by Dr. Emily Chang, the geologist in the group, is a demonstration of the mission's obligation to thorough investigation. The payload incorporates imaging frameworks, spectrometers, and land inspecting instruments, all intended for divulging the topographical secrets of Titan. Dr. Chang's skill in planetary topography guarantees that the Titan Explorer's logical instruments are streamlined for knowing the one of a kind elements of Titan's surface and sea depths.

The submarine's correspondence framework, planned by a group drove by Dr. Sophia Ramirez, guarantees consistent availability with mission control and the transmission of information back to Earth. The framework consolidates progressed signal handling strategies to defeat the difficulties presented by Titan's environmental circumstances, empowering constant correspondence and permitting researchers on Earth to direct the Titan Explorer through its investigation.

In the core of the Titan Explorer's war room, Authority James Mitchell, an accomplished space traveler, takes command of the submarine. His job isn't just to explore the submarine through Titan's many-sided territories yet in addition to go with constant choices in light of the information gathered. Leader Mitchell's mastery in space investigation and his capacity to adjust to the powerful difficulties of Titan make him a focal figure in the progress of the mission.

As the Titan Explorer gets ready for its plummet into Titan's subsurface sea, the expectation among the group is discernible. Dr. Marcus Thompson, the sea life researcher on the mission, supervises the organic investigation angles. The submarine is furnished with particular cameras and sensors intended to recognize expected indications of something going on under the surface in Titan's sea. Dr. Thompson's mastery in extremophiles on Earth illuminates the quest for extraordinary transformations and biochemistries that might exist in Titan's freezing, hydrocarbon-rich oceans.

The organization of the Titan Explorer is a demonstration of human inventiveness and the determined quest for information. The mission, directed by Dr. Victoria Hayes' initiative, addresses a cooperative exertion that pushes the limits of room investigation. The Titan Explorer, with its cutting edge innovation, epitomizes the aggregate skill of researchers, architects, and travelers who have met up to unwind the secrets of Titan and, likewise, the more extensive secrets of our nearby planet group.

As the Titan Explorer slips through Titan's climate, the group at mission control screens its encouraging with a mix of energy and dread. The sub's high level sensors begin catching information about Titan's surface elements, giving a see of the secrets anticipating investigation. The automated arms, under the deft control of Dr. Alan Rodriguez, go through beginning tests, exhibiting their versatility and accuracy.

The surface investigation period of the Titan Explorer permits researchers to concentrate on Titan's geography, environment, and sythesis in phenomenal detail. Dr. Emily Chang, examining the land information sent by the submarine, distinguishes likely destinations of interest for additional investigation. The Titan Explorer's portability on a superficial level, worked with by its impetus framework and mechanical arms, makes way for a thorough geographical overview.

The progress from the surface to the subsurface is a basic point for the Titan Explorer. Dr. Hayden Carter's impetus framework draws in consistently, working with the drop into Titan's sea. The group, drove by Commandant James Mitchell, guarantees that the sub's entrance into the fluid hydrocarbons is executed with accuracy. The drive framework's effectiveness is scrutinized as the Titan Explorer dives into the obscure profundities.

As the sub arrives at the sea depths, the Titan Explorer's automated arms become the overwhelming focus. Dr. Alan Rodriguez coordinates the perplexing dance of the mechanical limbs, directing them toward possible geographical developments.

The examining instruments, intended for Titan's interesting climate, gather examples that guarantee to open the land insider facts of Titan's subsurface. The group at mission control screens the mechanical moves with a feeling of expectation, anticipating the transmission of information from the sea depths.

Dr. Marcus Thompson, administering the organic investigation, coordinates the particular cameras toward areas of premium that might hold onto indications of something going on under the surface. The Titan Explorer's high level imaging frameworks catch the ethereal excellence of Titan's sea, uncovering a world washed in fluid hydrocarbons. Dr. Thompson's skill in sea life science illuminates the quest for potential biosignatures and transformations that might exist in this extraterrestrial biological system.

The Titan Explorer's correspondence framework, under the direction of Dr. Sophia Ramirez, works with the transmission of information back to Earth. The group of researchers anxiously anticipates the appearance of the principal pictures and estimations from the sub's investigation. Dr. Victoria Hayes, with a mix of energy and logical interest, drives the conversations at mission control, deciphering the information and forming speculations about Titan's subsurface climate.

As the Titan Explorer proceeds with its investigation, it experiences surprising varieties in the organization and temperature of the fluid hydrocarbons. Dr. Emily Chang, drawing on her geographical ability, teams up with Dr. Alan Rodriguez to adjust the automated arms' testing system continuously. The unique idea of the sea depths, with possible geothermal elements or hydrocarbon vents, adds layers to the logical story and prompts further examination.

The Titan Explorer, with its set-up of instruments and mechanical capacities, turns into a signal of development in the domain of room investigation. The submarine's versatility to the difficulties of Titan's current circumstance exhibits the potential for future missions to investigate different divine bodies. Dr. Hayes, in meetings and public locations, features the Titan Explorer as a demonstration of human interest and the ability to conquer the difficulties of investigating the vast unexplored world.

As the Titan Explorer finishes up its main goal and reemerges from Titan's sea, the group ponders the extraordinary excursion. The information gathered, the examples got, and the pictures caught illustrate Titan's interesting climate. The submarine's mechanical progressions, from its warm protection to its automated arms, prepare for future investigation tries in the external spans of our planetary group.

The Titan Explorer, in its presentation and investigation, turns out to be in excess of a logical instrument; it turns into an image of human accomplishment. Dr. Hayes, tending to the worldwide crowd, underlines the significance of pushing the limits of investigation and the potential for future missions to expand upon the tradition of the Titan Explorer.

The submarine's excursion, from conceptualization to execution, turns into a story of human creativity and the tenacious quest for information in the huge spread of the universe.

3.2 Highlight its advanced technology and capabilities for exploring Titan's ocean depths.

The trend setting innovation and capacities of the Titan Explorer stand as a demonstration of human creativity and the persistent quest for information in the domain of room investigation. Designed for the particular difficulties presented by Titan's moon, the submarine joins state of the art elements to explore and investigate the sea profundities of this far off divine body. From its vigorous outside to its modern instrumentation, the Titan Explorer represents the zenith of development in extraterrestrial investigation.

At the bleeding edge of the Titan Explorer's trend setting innovation is its warm protection, an essential component intended to endure the super cool common on Titan. The moon's surface temperature floats around - 290 degrees Fahrenheit (- 179 degrees Celsius), making it perhaps of the coldest climate in our planetary group. To counter these freezing conditions, the Titan Explorer's external shell consolidates cutting edge protection materials that guarantee the submarine remaining parts functional in the cruel and cold climate.

The protection isn't just a defensive hindrance yet in addition an essential component in enhancing the sub's presentation. Dr. Victoria Hayes, the head of the mission, accentuates the meaning of this component, noticing that it permits the Titan Explorer to persevere through delayed openness to Titan's freezing temperatures, working with expanded investigation and information assortment. The protection turns into a safeguard against the unforgiving components of the moon, empowering the sub to explore its surface and dive into its subsurface sea with versatility.

One more weighty part of the Titan Explorer's innovation lies in its impetus framework, designed under the direction of Dr. Hayden Carter. The drive framework is fundamental for exploring Titan's environment, arriving at the surface, and leading exact moves both ashore and in the fluid hydrocarbon oceans. Dr. Carter's group has created impetus instruments that balance proficiency, accuracy, and flexibility, permitting the sub to navigate Titan's different territories with deftness.

The Titan Explorer's plunge into Titan's subsurface sea is a basic period of the mission, requiring an impetus framework that can change consistently from environmental section to submerged investigation. The innovation consolidated in this impetus framework works with controlled plunges, empowering the sub to arrive at the sea depths with accuracy. The progress of the Titan Explorer in moving through Titan's air and investigating its sea profundities is a demonstration of the complexity of its drive innovation.

Vital to the sub's logical capacities are its automated arms, a many-sided piece of designing drove by Dr. Alan Rodriguez. The mechanical arms are furnished with accuracy instruments, sensors, and inspecting systems intended to cooperate with Titan's different territories, from frosty fields to the sea depths. Dr. Rodriguez's mastery in advanced mechanics guarantees that the Titan Explorer's arms are versatile as well as receptive to the powerful difficulties experienced during the mission.

The mechanical arms assume a urgent part in example assortment and examination, expanding the span of the Titan Explorer to places unavailable to different instruments. Dr. Rodriguez's group has planned these arms to carefully explore through Titan's outsider climate, acclimating to the changing structures of the moon's surface and subsurface. The versatility of the mechanical arms permits the Titan Explorer to direct land studies, gather examples, and add to the exhaustive investigation of Titan's extraordinary elements.

As the Titan Explorer plunges into the subsurface sea, the automated arms stretch out into the fluid hydrocarbons, gathering tests from the sea floor. The accuracy with which these examining moves are executed is a consequence of Dr. Rodriguez's careful designing and the high level capacities of the automated arms. The gathered examples hold the commitment of opening the geographical and possibly natural mysteries disguised in Titan's sea profundities.

Dr. Emily Chang, the geologist on the mission, uses the Titan Explorer's logical payload to concentrate on the land elements of Titan's surface and sea floor. The payload incorporates imaging frameworks, spectrometers, and geographical examining instruments, each adding to an extensive examination of Titan's one of a kind climate. Dr. Chang's mastery in planetary geography guarantees that the Titan Explorer's logical instruments are advanced for knowing the topographical secrets of Titan.

The imaging frameworks catch high-goal pictures of Titan's surface, giving nitty gritty guides of its geology. These pictures, combined with spectrometric information, empower researchers to investigate the sythesis of Titan's surface materials. Dr. Chang's group works together with Dr. Rodriguez to connect land highlights with mechanical arm inspecting, making a comprehensive comprehension of Titan's subsurface climate. The Titan Explorer's logical payload, upgraded by cutting edge imaging and spectroscopy innovations, turns into a useful asset for unwinding the land complexities of Titan.

The Titan Explorer's correspondence framework, planned by Dr. Sophia Ramirez, is one more basic part that guarantees consistent availability with mission control and the transmission of information back to Earth. Correspondence with a sub investigating the profundities of an extraterrestrial sea presents remarkable difficulties, given the states of Titan's environment. Dr. Ramirez's group has executed progressed signal handling procedures to defeat these difficulties, permitting ongoing correspondence and information transmission.

The correspondence framework works with a nonstop trade of data between the Titan Explorer and mission control, giving researchers bits of knowledge into the continuous investigation. Dr. Ramirez's skill in signal handling guarantees that the Titan Explorer's information transmissions stay clear and dependable regardless of the climatic states of Titan. This continuous correspondence capacity empowers researchers on Earth to direct the sub through its investigation and settle on informed choices in view of the information got.

The organic investigation part of the Titan Explorer, regulated by Dr. Marcus Thompson, is a demonstration of the sub's flexibility in concentrating on expected indications of something going on under the surface. Specific cameras and sensors intended for natural identification are incorporated into the Titan Explorer's logical payload. Dr. Thompson's ability in sea life science illuminates the quest for biosignatures and transformations that might exist in Titan's cold, hydrocarbon-rich oceans.

The Titan Explorer's cameras catch high-goal pictures of the sea floor, uncovering the many-sided elements of Titan's outsider climate. Dr. Thompson's group breaks down these pictures for any indications of development, structures, or different markers that might recommend the presence of life. The high level imaging innovation integrated into the sub's plan improves the probability of distinguishing organic peculiarities that could have in any case stayed secret in Titan's sea profundities.

The flexibility of the Titan Explorer, displayed through its double usefulness for surface and subsurface investigation, is a sign of its trend setting innovation. The submarine consistently advances between climatic passage, surface route, and subsurface investigation, showing its capacity to investigate different territories on Titan. Dr. Victoria Hayes highlights the significance of this adaptability in amplifying the logical return of the mission and making ready for future investigation tries.

The Titan Explorer's trend setting innovation and capacities have expansive ramifications for the eventual fate of room investigation. Dr. Hayes, in meetings and public locations, stresses the Titan Explorer's job as a pioneer in the journey to figure out the planetary group's external scopes. The sub's progress in exploring Titan's sea profundities features the potential for comparative missions to investigate the subsurface expanses of other heavenly bodies, opening new roads for the quest for life past Earth.

In the finishing up periods of its main goal, as the Titan Explorer reemerges from Titan's sea, the group ponders the abundance of information, tests, and pictures gathered. The submarine's process turns into a story of win, not simply as far as the logical disclosures made yet in addition in pushing the limits of mechanical development. The Titan Explorer, with its trend setting innovation and capacities, makes a permanent imprint on the continuous adventure of human investigation, motivating future missions to disentangle the secrets of the universe.

As the Titan Explorer restores correspondence with mission control, the group praises the effective execution of a remarkable investigation mission. Dr. Hayes, tending to the worldwide crowd, features the cooperative endeavors that finished in the Titan Explorer's accomplishments. The trend setting innovation and abilities of the submarine, joined with the skill of the different group, represent the human ability to beat difficulties and investigate the astronomical unexplored world.

The tradition of the Titan Explorer reaches out past the limits of Titan's moon. Dr. Hayes imagines the submarine as a venturing stone for future missions to investigate the subsurface expanses of frosty moons around gas monsters, like Europa and Enceladus. The examples gained from the Titan Explorer's process will educate the plan and execution regarding ensuing missions, impelling humankind further into the investigation of extraterrestrial seas and the quest for life past our home planet.

In the records of room investigation, the Titan Explorer remains as an image of mechanical ability and logical interest. The sub's investigation of Titan's sea profundities adds to our advancing comprehension of the nearby planet group and the possible livability of far off moons. The Titan Explorer's excursion, from its conceptualization to its victorious investigation, rouses another age of researchers, specialists, and pilgrims to push the limits of information and set out on journeys that challenge the constraints of human creativity.

3.3 Engineers and scientists fine-tune the submersible for the challenging mission.

The tweaking of the sub for the difficult mission on Titan's maritime profundities addresses a critical stage in the Sub Stories Titan's Maritime Investigation. As the interdisciplinary group of specialists and researchers collects to set up the Titan Explorer for its extraordinary excursion, a cooperative exertion results to enhance the submarine's plan, instrumentation, and functional capacities.

Driven by Dr. Victoria Hayes, a visionary researcher intensely for unwinding the secrets of the planetary group, the group leaves on the mind boggling course of refining the Titan Explorer for the novel difficulties presented by Titan, Saturn's biggest moon. The mission's prosperity depends on the fastidious tender loving care during the tweaking stage, where every part and framework is investigated and acclimated to guarantee the sub's flexibility and versatility.

The architects, under the administration of Dr. Hayden Carter, start the calibrating system by zeroing in on the impetus framework — a basic component for exploring Titan's climate and progressing from surface to subsurface investigation.

The difficulties introduced by Titan's thick air and different territories require an impetus framework that can work with accuracy and productivity. Dr. Carter's group conducts broad reenactments and tests to enhance the submarine's drive, guaranteeing it can execute complex moves expected for the mission's prosperity.

At the same time, Dr. Alan Rodriguez, the roboticist managing the mission's mechanical parts, adjusts the automated arms that are necessary to the Titan Explorer's investigation capacities. These mechanical extremities, furnished with cutting edge sensors and inspecting devices, go through acclimations to upgrade their versatility to Titan's outsider climate. Dr. Rodriguez teams up with the designing group to synchronize the mechanical arms with the impetus framework, making a consistent reconciliation that permits the submarine to explore and gather tests really.

The correspondence framework, initiated by Dr. Sophia Ramirez, goes through careful calibrating to guarantee solid availability between the Titan Explorer and mission control on The planet. Titan's barometrical circumstances, particular from those experienced in past space missions, present correspondence challenges that request imaginative arrangements. Dr. Ramirez's group executes signal handling strategies and improvements to defeat the potential interruptions brought about by Titan's thick air, guaranteeing a steady and nonstop trade of information.

As the architects refine the specialized parts of the submarine, the logical group, drove by Dr. Emily Chang, centers around tweaking the payload — a set-up of instruments intended to catch a far reaching dataset from Titan's surface and subsurface. The imaging frameworks, spectrometers, and land examining apparatuses are aligned to amplify their adequacy in the extraterrestrial climate. Dr. Chang teams up with the designing and mechanical groups to synchronize the logical payload with the general mission targets.

The cooperative endeavors reach out to the functional parts of the mission, where Leader James Mitchell, an accomplished space explorer, assumes a focal part. Commandant Mitchell, administering the mix of the designing and logical parts, adjusts the functional conventions for the Titan Explorer. Mimicked missions and situation based preparing become fundamental devices to guarantee the group's availability to address unanticipated difficulties during the genuine investigation.

In the core of the mission control focus, situated on The planet, the group accumulates for complete briefings and recreations. Dr. Victoria Hayes, with a mix of logical excitement and key prescience, directs the group through the complexities of the mission. The calibrating stage turns into a unique course of iterative changes, with every reproduction giving important bits of knowledge that add to the refinement of the submarine's plan and functional conventions.

As the group tweaks the Titan Explorer, outside variables like financing requirements, strategic contemplations, and the developing comprehension of Titan's current circumstance become an integral factor. Dr. Hayes, adroit at exploring both the logical and authoritative parts of the mission, guarantees that the tweaking system stays lined up with the all-encompassing objectives of the Submarine Stories Titan's Maritime Investigation.

The coordinated effort among designers and researchers turns into a sign of the calibrating stage, cultivating a cross-disciplinary trade of thoughts and skill. Dr. Emily Chang's land experiences impact acclimations to the mechanical arms' examining systems, while Dr. Hayden Carter's drive enhancements consider the potential land highlights distinguished by the logical group. The collaboration between the specialized and logical parts of the mission turns into a main impetus behind the progress of the tweaking system.

As the Titan Explorer goes through conclusive arrangements, the group faces unanticipated difficulties that require creative arrangements. Dr. Alan Rodriguez, confronted with surprising varieties in Titan's barometrical circumstances during re-productions, drives the advancement of versatile calculations for the mechanical arms. These calculations permit the mechanical limbs to progressively answer changing natural variables, exhibiting the group's nimbleness in tending to constant difficulties.

The tweaking stage likewise incorporates a progression of emergency courses of action, perceiving that the unusualness of room investigation requests a readiness for the unforeseen. Dr. Victoria Hayes, underscoring the significance of flexibility and versatility, directs the group in creating reaction procedures for possible peculiarities, framework disappointments, or deviations from the mission plan. The thorough way to deal with tweaking incorporates upgrading execution as well as getting ready for the vulnerabilities that characterize investigation past Earth.

As the Titan Explorer approaches its day for kickoff, the group considers the groundbreaking excursion of adjusting the sub for Titan's maritime investigation. The mission's prosperity depends on mechanical ability as well as on the cooperative soul that joins researchers and designers in a common quest for disclosure. Dr. Hayes, tending to the group in a pre-send off instructions, praises the aggregate exertion that has carried the Titan Explorer from conceptualization to a finely tuned instrument of extraterrestrial investigation.

The send off day shows up, denoting the summit of long stretches of calibrating, coordinated effort, and readiness. The Titan Explorer, with its upgraded impetus framework, adjusted logical payload, and versatile mechanical arms, stands prepared for the remarkable mission into Titan's maritime profundities. The group at mission control screens the sub's rising into space, a second that typifies the aggregate commitment and skill that characterize the Sub Stories Titan's Maritime Investigation.

As the Titan Explorer leaves on its interplanetary excursion, the group stays watchful, prepared to answer the unique difficulties that anticipate. Dr. Victoria Hayes, noticing the send off with a feeling of expectation, considers the tweaking stage as a demonstration of human inventiveness and the dauntless soul of investigation. The Sub Stories Titan's Maritime Investigation, with its finely tuned sub, turns into a reference point of motivation for people in the future of researchers and wayfarers, welcoming them to drive the limits of information and adventure into the grandiose unexplored world.

Chapter 4

Launch and Descent

The summit of fastidious preparation, designing artfulness, and logical expectation, the send off of the Titan Explorer denotes the inception of an earth shattering mission — Sub Stories Titan's Maritime Investigation. As the submarine leaves the bounds of Earth's air, setting out on an excursion toward Saturn's biggest moon, Titan, the aggregate endeavors of researchers, specialists, and travelers meet in a second that resounds with the soul of human interest and the quest for information.

In the mission control focus, an unmistakable demeanor of fervor pervades the room as the Titan Explorer takes off from Earth. Dr. Victoria Hayes, the visionary researcher driving the mission, notices the send off with a combination of pride and expectation. The send off vehicle, impelled by a strong rocket, conveys the Titan Explorer on a direction that will eventually lead it to the far off moon of Saturn. The group at mission control, included researchers, specialists, and care staff, screens each phase of the send off with resolute concentration.

Leader James Mitchell, an accomplished space explorer in charge of the Titan Explorer, takes command of the submarine as it isolates from the send off vehicle.

The excursion to Titan is a mind boggling dance through the infinite expressive dance of divine bodies, and Commandant Mitchell explores the sub with accuracy, guaranteeing it follows the determined direction toward its objective. The drive framework, adjusted during the mission's readiness stage, pushes the Titan Explorer through the huge span of room.

The excursion to Titan isn't without its difficulties. The group at mission control screens the sub's advancement, changing course depending on the situation to represent gravitational powers and other divine elements. Dr. Hayden Carter, the specialist liable for the drive framework, teams up with Leader Mitchell to execute direction changes, guaranteeing the Titan Explorer stays on track for its noteworthy meeting with Titan.

As the Titan Explorer moves toward Saturn's framework, the group plans for the plummet into Titan's environment — a basic stage that requires exact route and execution. The thick environment of Titan presents difficulties unmistakable from those experienced in past space investigation missions. Dr. Hayden Carter's drive framework, tried and adjusted during reproductions, draws in with accuracy, permitting the sub to penetrate through Titan's barometrical shroud.

The plummet through Titan's air is a tactile encounter for the group at mission control. The sub experiences the barometrical layers, with the encompassing cloudiness steadily giving approach to looks at Titan's surface. Dr. Emily Chang, the geologist on the mission, centers around the underlying pictures and information communicated by the Titan Explorer's sensors. The surface highlights become detectable, uncovering a scene set apart by huge hills and strange pools of fluid hydrocarbons.

The drive framework, a wonder of designing inventiveness, changes with the air conditions, guaranteeing a controlled plummet. Dr. Hayden Carter and Authority James Mitchell team up progressively to enhance the sub's direction, taking into account the developing climatic elements. The group's capacity to adjust to the unique difficulties of Titan's drop highlights the interdisciplinary joint effort that characterizes the mission.

As the Titan Explorer infiltrates further into Titan's air, the group faces the following period of the plunge — the passage into the moon's subsurface sea. Dr. Alan Rodriguez, administering the mechanical arms, arranges their withdrawal to get ready for the looming change from barometrical section to amphibian investigation. The mechanical arms, furnished with examining devices and sensors, will assume a crucial part in gathering information and tests from Titan's sea floor.

The climatic passage into Titan's sea is a snapshot of expectation and misgiving. Dr. Marcus Thompson, the sea life scientist on the mission, screens the Titan Explorer's instruments for any indications of something going on under the surface as it plummets into the fluid hydrocarbons.

The submarine, intended for double usefulness in both surface and subsurface investigation, is currently ready to unwind the secrets disguised underneath the cold covering of Titan's confounding sea.

As the Titan Explorer enters the fluid hydrocarbons, the group encounters a progress from the known to the unexplored world. The mechanical arms, under the direction of Dr. Alan Rodriguez, stretch out into the sea, prepared to investigate the sea floor. The group at mission control, eagerly, anticipates the transmission of information and pictures that will give experiences into the insider facts concealed underneath Titan's cold oceans.

The Titan Explorer, presently in the subsurface sea, turns into a trailblazer in extraterrestrial oceanic investigation. Dr. Marcus Thompson coordinates the particular cameras toward likely organic areas of interest, while Dr. Emily Chang centers around geographical arrangements that might hold pieces of information to Titan's land history. The sub's plunge into the sea floor turns into a journey of revelation, offering a brief look into an outsider climate that has stayed disguised underneath the cold surface of Titan.

Dr. Victoria Hayes, tending to the group at mission control, recognizes the noteworthy idea existing apart from everything else. The Titan Explorer, with its trend setting innovation and capacities, has effectively explored the difficulties of send off, climatic section, and plummet. The cooperative endeavors of researchers and designers have carried humankind really close to uncovering the secrets that exist in Titan's subsurface sea — an achievement that reverberates with the soul of investigation that characterizes our species.

The investigation of Titan's sea depths is led with fastidious accuracy. The automated arms, under the direction of Dr. Alan Rodriguez, gather tests and direct investigations, uncovering the organization and topographical highlights of Titan's subsurface climate. Dr. Emily Chang's geographical ability comes to the front as the Titan Explorer researches potential areas of interest that could give bits of knowledge into the moon's land advancement.

The specific cameras, intended for organic investigation under the oversight of Dr. Marcus Thompson, catch pictures of Titan's submerged domain. The group examines the recording for any indications of something going on under the surface or one of a kind variations that might exist in this hydrocarbon-rich climate. The Titan Explorer's central goal stretches out past the domain of planetary geography, wandering into the domain of astrobiology as it looks for potential biosignatures.

As the Titan Explorer proceeds with its investigation, the group faces startling peculiarities that add layers to the mission's story. Unidentified designs on the sea depths, odd varieties in temperature, and baffling geographical developments brief the group to rethink how they might interpret Titan's subsurface climate.

Dr. Chang, drawing on her geographical mastery, drives the group in unraveling the ramifications of these revelations, perceiving that Titan's secrets reach out past the expected.

The surprising difficulties and revelations just strengthen the logical talk encompassing the Titan Explorer. Mainstream researchers, once incredulous, ends up brought into the unfurling account of the mission. The group's devotion to thorough logical request, combined with their capacity to adjust to unexpected conditions, earns regard and backing from their companions.

The Titan Explorer, in its main goal to investigate the known and obscure parts of Titan's novel climate, turns into an image of human creativity and assurance. Dr. Hayes, pondering the excursion, discusses the mission's heritage stretching out past the quick logical revelations. The Titan Explorer, through its investigation of Titan's sea, rouses another age of researchers and pilgrims to push the limits of information and embrace the difficulties of the inestimable unexplored world.

As the mission moves toward its decision, the group assembles for a post-op interview, considering the groundbreaking excursion into Titan's sea. The Submarine: Titan Explorer, once met with incredulity, has effectively explored the intricacies of an exceptional mission, making a permanent imprint on the continuous adventure of human investigation. The revelations made, the difficulties survive, and the illustrations learned become piece of the logical story, adding to humankind's aggregate comprehension of the secrets that plague our nearby planet group.

The tradition of the Submarine: Titan Explorer, with its known and obscure disclosures, resounded through the hallways of logical establishments and reverberated with the more extensive public. Dr. Hayes, tending to the worldwide crowd in a closing explanation, underscored the significance of interest driven investigation in growing the wildernesses of human information. The Titan Explorer, in its journey to figure out Titan's sea, turned into a reference point of motivation, welcoming humankind to focus on the stars and dream of the secrets ready to be revealed in the grandiose expanse of conceivable outcomes.

4.1 The team launches Titan Voyager into space.

The pivotal send off of the Titan Explorer into space denotes the commencement of a logical odyssey that rises above the limits of Earth, wandering into the perplexing domain of Saturn's biggest moon, Titan. Driven by the visionary researcher, Dr. Victoria Hayes, a different and interdisciplinary group of designers, researchers, and wayfarers teams up to move mankind into the unfamiliar regions of extraterrestrial maritime investigation.

The mission's send off fills in as a demonstration of the aggregate exertion and resourcefulness put resources into the Titan Explorer.

As the sub leaves on its interplanetary excursion, the group at mission control, an operational hub of logical coordination, screens the takeoff with a mix of fervor and expectation. The Titan Explorer's send off vehicle, a transcending demonstration of human designing, impels the sub past the bounds of Earth's climate, making way for an uncommon investigation mission.

Dr. Victoria Hayes, the main impetus behind the Sub Stories Titan's Maritime Investigation, watches the send off with a combination of pride and logical energy. The summit of long stretches of arranging, improvement, and testing, the Titan Explorer isn't just a vehicle however a harbinger of revelation — a course through which mankind looks to disentangle the secrets of Titan's subsurface sea. Dr. Hayes tends to the group, stressing the authentic meaning of this second and the potential for noteworthy disclosures that lie ahead.

Administrator James Mitchell, an accomplished space traveler chose to steerage the Titan Explorer, takes command of the submarine as it isolates from the send off vehicle. The change from the World's air to the enormous span is a sensitive dance directed by accuracy and determined directions. Commandant Mitchell, in a joint effort with the designing group drove by Dr. Hayden Carter, arranges the moves that drive the Titan Explorer on its direction toward Saturn and its fascinating moon.

The impetus framework, a wonder of designing inventiveness tweaked during broad reproductions and tests, pushes the Titan Explorer through the immensity of room. Dr. Hayden Carter's mastery in impetus becomes central as the submarine explores the complex gravitational fields and directions that characterize interplanetary travel.

The impetus framework's productivity and versatility become vital in guaranteeing the Titan Explorer's fruitful excursion toward its extraterrestrial objective.

As the Titan Explorer navigates the grandiose field, the group at mission control screens the all sub's moves, expecting the difficulties that lie ahead. Dr. Alan Rodriguez, the roboticist supervising the mission's mechanical parts, guarantees that the automated arms, outfitted with accuracy devices and sensors, are prepared for their job in the investigation of Titan's maritime profundities. The cooperative collaboration between the designing and logical groups becomes clear as the Titan Explorer advances toward its objective.

The excursion toward Titan includes exploring the intricacies of the nearby planet group, representing gravitational impacts, orbital elements, and the immense distances that different divine bodies. Dr. Sophia Ramirez, liable for the correspondence framework, assumes a basic part in keeping a consistent association between the Titan Explorer and mission control. The correspondence framework, exposed to the difficulties of room travel, depends on cutting edge signal handling and hand-off instruments to guarantee the consistent progression of information.

As the Titan Explorer moves toward Saturn's framework, the group gets ready for the following significant stage — the plunge toward Titan. Dr. Emily Chang, the geologist driving the logical undertakings, centers around the arrangements for climatic section. The thick air of Titan, particular from Earth's, requires exact computations and changes in accordance with the plunge direction. Dr. Chang teams up with Administrator Mitchell to guarantee that the Titan Explorer's entrance into Titan's air is executed with accuracy.

The environmental passage turns into a basic crossroads in the mission, with the Titan Explorer encountering the opposition and elements of Titan's thick air. The group at mission control, collaborating with Authority Mitchell, screens the drop and makes constant acclimations to explore through the barometrical layers. The Titan Explorer punctures through the barometrical cloak, uncovering looks at Titan's surface highlights — a preface to the investigation that anticipates in the moon's subsurface sea.

The plunge proceeds, directed by the fastidiously calibrated drive framework. Dr. Hayden Carter, as a team with Commandant Mitchell, guarantees that the sub changes flawlessly from air passage to the following period of its excursion — the investigation of Titan's surface and inevitable drop into its subsurface sea. The group's capacity to adjust to the unique difficulties of Titan's air highlights the versatility and accuracy of the designing and functional parts.

As the Titan Explorer moves toward the surface, the group observers Titan's outsider scenes unfurl — a territory set apart by transcending rises, immense fields, and secretive pools of fluid hydrocarbons. Dr. Emily Chang, immediately taking advantage of the chance introduced by the Titan Explorer's surface investigation abilities, guides the logical payload to catch high-goal pictures and gather introductory information about Titan's geography. The Titan Explorer's mechanical arms, under the direction of Dr. Alan Rodriguez, stand prepared for their job in the thorough investigation of Titan's surface.

The Titan Explorer's underlying surface investigation turns into an introduction to the inescapable drop into Titan's subsurface sea. The group, floated by the outcome of the environmental section and surface investigation, gets ready for the following period of the mission. Dr. Marcus Thompson, the sea life researcher directing the organic investigation part, centers around the specific cameras and sensors intended to distinguish possible indications of something going on under the surface in Titan's maritime profundities.

Leader James Mitchell, in charge of the Titan Explorer, starts the plunge into Titan's subsurface sea — a snapshot of extraordinary expectation for the whole group. The drive framework, a workhorse all through the excursion, draws in with accuracy to work with the controlled plummet. The change from Titan's surface to its subsurface climate requires consistent coordination between the impetus framework, mechanical arms, and logical payload — a demonstration of the mix of designing and logical skill.

The Titan Explorer's drop into the subsurface sea turns into an extraordinary second in the mission. The group at mission control screens the plunge with a mix of fervor and worry, mindful that the sub is very nearly entering an extraterrestrial sea up until recently never investigated by human innovation. The group's aggregate center escalates as the Titan Explorer dives into the fluid hydrocarbons that cover the insider facts of Titan's subsurface.

As the Titan Explorer lowers into the sea, the group changes into a method of centered expectation. Dr. Alan Rodriguez assumes control over the automated arms, organizing their organization into the fluid hydrocarbons. The automated members, outfitted with specific testing devices and sensors, stretch out into the sea, prepared to investigate the sea floor and gather tests that might hold the way in to Titan's land and possibly organic secrets.

Dr. Marcus Thompson, supervising the natural investigation, coordinates the particular cameras toward areas of premium that might hold onto indications of something going on under the surface. The Titan Explorer's high level imaging frameworks catch the ethereal magnificence of Titan's sea, uncovering a world washed in fluid hydrocarbons. Dr. Thompson's aptitude in sea life science illuminates the quest for potential biosignatures and variations that might exist in this extraterrestrial environment.

The Titan Explorer's correspondence framework, under the direction of Dr. Sophia Ramirez, works with the transmission of information back to Earth. The group of researchers enthusiastically anticipates the appearance of the primary pictures and estimations from the submarine's investigation. Dr. Victoria Hayes, with a mix of fervor and logical interest, drives the conversations at mission control, deciphering the information and figuring out speculations about Titan's subsurface climate.

As the Titan Explorer proceeds with its investigation, it experiences surprising varieties in the piece and temperature of the fluid hydrocarbons. Dr. Emily Chang, drawing on her topographical aptitude, teams up with Dr. Alan Rodriguez to break down the information and pictures sent by the submarine. The startling geographical highlights on the sea floor brief the group to rethink how they might interpret Titan's subsurface climate, stressing the powerful idea of extraterrestrial investigation.

The Titan Explorer's mechanical arms, controlled with accuracy by Dr. Alan Rodriguez and his group, gather tests from the sea depths. The topographical and possibly organic examples become a gold mine of information that holds the commitment of disentangling Titan's puzzling secrets. Dr. Marcus Thompson, breaking down the natural information, examines the pictures for any indications of development or designs that might show the presence of life in Titan's sea.

The group, directed by Dr. Victoria Hayes' essential authority, adjusts to the surprising difficulties and disclosures, changing each obstacle into a chance for logical request. The mission's prosperity isn't just characterized by the affirmation of assumptions yet by the readiness of the group to embrace the obscure and investigate the unfamiliar regions of Titan's sea.

As the Titan Explorer proceeds with its investigation, the group at mission control thinks about the groundbreaking idea of the mission. The subsurface: Titan Explorer, once met with distrust, has turned into a pioneer in the journey for extraterrestrial life and topographical comprehension. The cooperative endeavors of researchers and specialists, under the visionary direction of Dr. Victoria Hayes, have impelled mankind into the front of room investigation.

The Titan Explorer's excursion into Titan's sea turns into an image of human resourcefulness, assurance, and the determined quest for information. The group, as a team with the complex innovation incorporated into the sub, has effectively explored the difficulties of room travel, barometrical section, surface investigation, and subsurface plummet. The Titan Explorer remains as a guide of motivation for people in the future, empowering them to investigate the vast obscure and push the limits of human getting it.

4.2 The journey to Titan and the tense descent into the moon's atmosphere.

The excursion to Titan, Saturn's biggest moon, addresses an extraordinary journey for the Titan Explorer — a refined submarine outfitted with cutting edge innovation and a logical payload intended to investigate the moon's baffling subsurface sea. Driven by Dr. Victoria Hayes, a visionary researcher enthusiastically for unwinding the secrets of the nearby planet group, the interdisciplinary group of specialists, researchers, and travelers sets out on an excursion that rises above the limits of Earth.

The send off from Earth is a snapshot of aggregate expectation and pride for the group. The Titan Explorer, settled inside its send off vehicle, ascends from the surface, moved by strong rockets that convey it past the World's air. Dr. Victoria Hayes, in charge of the mission, watches the takeoff with a mix of logical interest and a feeling of obligation. The Titan Explorer isn't simply a shuttle; it is a vessel of human resourcefulness and an image of the unquenchable human longing to investigate the grandiose unexplored world.

As the Titan Explorer ventures through the boundlessness of room, the group at mission control screens its direction and changes course depending on the situation. Dr. Hayden Carter, the designer answerable for the impetus framework, teams up with Administrator James Mitchell to enhance the submarine's way through the divine field. The Titan Explorer's drive framework, calibrated during reenactments and tests, exhibits its flexibility as it impels the submarine toward Saturn and its charming moon, Titan.

The correspondence framework, administered by Dr. Sophia Ramirez, assumes a critical part in keeping a consistent connection between the Titan Explorer and mission control. Titan's exceptional climatic circumstances present correspondence challenges not experienced in past space missions, requiring creative arrangements. Dr. Ramirez and her group execute signal handling strategies to guarantee a steady and nonstop trade of information, conquering the obstacles presented by Titan's thick environment.

As the Titan Explorer moves toward Saturn's framework, the group plans for the strained plummet into Titan's environment — a basic stage that requests accuracy and flexibility. Dr. Emily Chang, the geologist driving the logical undertakings, centers around the barometrical passage, perceiving the exceptional difficulties introduced by Titan's thick air. The plummet is a snapshot of union for the designing and logical groups, where their cooperative endeavors should synchronize to explore the intricacies of Titan's air elements.

Leader James Mitchell, an accomplished space explorer with a background marked by space missions, takes command of the Titan Explorer during the drop. The impetus framework, directed by Dr. Hayden Carter's skill, draws in with accuracy to work with a controlled passage into Titan's air. The group at mission control, including architects, researchers, and care staff, watches eagerly as the sub starts its drop, directed by the zenith of long periods of arranging, reproductions, and calibrating.

The climatic section into Titan is a tactile encounter for the group at mission control. The Titan Explorer experiences the layers of Titan's thick air, with the encompassing murkiness step by step giving approach to looks at Titan's surface. Dr. Emily Chang, with her geographical ability, deciphers the underlying pictures and information sent by the Titan Explorer's sensors. The surface highlights become perceivable, uncovering a scene portrayed by transcending hills and pools of fluid hydrocarbons.

The impetus framework, an innovative wonder intended for the particular difficulties of Titan's environment, goes through continuous changes. Dr. Hayden Carter and Leader James Mitchell team up to enhance the sub's direction, guaranteeing a consistent progress from climatic section to the investigation of Titan's surface. The Titan Explorer's capacity to explore through Titan's climatic intricacies highlights the viability of the designing arrangements carried out by the group.

The plunge proceeds, with the Titan Explorer exploring through the unique layers of Titan's air. Dr. Emily Chang guides the logical payload to catch high-goal pictures and gather information about Titan's surface elements. The mechanical arms, under the direction of Dr. Alan Rodriguez, stand prepared for their job in the thorough investigation of Titan's surface. The group's capacity to adjust to the developing air conditions turns into a demonstration of their cooperative soul and readiness for the difficulties of extraterrestrial investigation.

As the Titan Explorer moves toward Titan's surface, the group observers the outsider scenes unfurl before their eyes. Dr. Emily Chang's land bits of knowledge guide the logical investigation, with the automated arms ready to collaborate with Titan's one of a kind territory. The Titan Explorer catches pictures of huge fields, transcending rises, and pools of fluid hydrocarbons — highlights that challenge assumptions and develop the interest encompassing Titan's geography.

The progress from climatic passage to surface investigation turns into a consistent dance among innovation and logical request. The Titan Explorer, outfitted with state of the art instruments, turns into mankind's eyes and hands on Titan's surface. Dr. Alan Rodriguez, directing the mechanical arms, organizes their developments as they interface with the landscape, gathering tests and leading geographical investigations. The information communicated back to mission control turns into a store of data that will shape's comprehension mankind might interpret Titan's surface and illuminate future investigation missions.

The Titan Explorer's effective investigation of Titan's surface denotes a critical achievement in the mission. The group at mission control, directed by Dr. Victoria Hayes' essential administration, praises the accomplishments of the plummet stage. The submarine's capacity to explore through Titan's barometrical difficulties and direct surface investigation exhibits the cooperative collaboration among designing and logical ability. Dr. Hayes, tending to the group, recognizes the meaning existing apart from everything else and underlines the significance of the impending stage — the plunge into Titan's subsurface sea.

The group changes its concentration to the following basic period of the mission — the plummet into Titan's subsurface sea. Dr. Marcus Thompson, the sea life scholar answerable for the natural investigation part, gets ready for the arrangement of specific cameras and sensors intended to recognize likely indications of something going on under the surface in Titan's maritime profundities. The Titan Explorer, having effectively explored climatic passage and surface investigation, is presently ready to reveal the secrets covered underneath the frosty outside of Titan's perplexing sea.

Commandant James Mitchell assumes control over the Titan Explorer, starting the plummet into Titan's subsurface sea — a snapshot of incredible expectation and strain. The impetus framework, under the careful oversight of Dr. Hayden Carter, draws in with accuracy to work with the controlled plunge into the fluid hydrocarbons that cover Titan's subsurface. The group at mission control screens the drop with centered consideration, mindful that the Titan Explorer is nearly entering a strange area.

The Titan Explorer's drop into the subsurface sea addresses an extraordinary second in the mission. The fluid hydrocarbons, in contrast to any natural climate, present special difficulties and open doors for investigation.

Dr. Alan Rodriguez, regulating the mechanical arms, coordinates their sending into the sea, prepared to collaborate with the sea depths, gather tests, and direct logical investigations. The group, with a feeling of expectation and logical interest, anticipates the transmission of information that will give bits of knowledge into the insider facts concealed underneath Titan's freezing oceans.

As the Titan Explorer lowers into the sea, the group at mission control encounters a change in center from environmental elements to oceanic investigation. Dr. Marcus Thompson coordinates the specific cameras toward expected organic areas of interest, while Dr. Emily Chang centers around land developments that might hold hints to Titan's geographical history. The Titan Explorer's excursion into the subsurface sea turns into a journey of disclosure, offering a brief look into an outsider climate that has stayed disguised underneath the frosty surface of Titan.

Dr. Sophia Ramirez, directing the correspondence framework, guarantees the continuous progression of information between the Titan Explorer and mission control. Titan's novel barometrical circumstances and the progress from surface to subsurface investigation request a solid and versatile correspondence framework. Dr. Ramirez's skill in signal handling and correspondence innovation becomes fundamental as the group depends on a steady stream of data to direct the sub through Titan's maritime profundities.

The Titan Explorer's plunge into the subsurface sea unfurls with a feeling of investigation and logical request. The mechanical arms, under the direction of Dr. Alan Rodriguez, gather tests from the sea depths, uncovering the organization and topographical highlights of Titan's subsurface climate. Dr. Emily Chang's topographical ability becomes instrumental in unraveling the meaning of the sea floor developments, revealing insight into Titan's geographical advancement.

Dr. Marcus Thompson, zeroing in on the natural investigation, examines the pictures caught by the particular cameras for any indications of something going on under the surface or exceptional transformations that might exist in this hydrocarbon-rich climate. The Titan Explorer's central goal stretches out past the domain of planetary geography, wandering into the domain of astrobiology as it looks for potential biosignatures. The group's aggregate consideration goes to the chance of revealing signs about the expected presence of extraterrestrial life in Titan's subsurface sea.

As the Titan Explorer proceeds with its investigation, unforeseen peculiarities and disclosures arise. Unidentified designs on the sea depths, atypical varieties in temperature, and perplexing geographical developments brief the group to reevaluate how they might interpret Titan's subsurface climate. Dr. Chang, drawing on her land mastery, drives the group in unraveling the ramifications of these revelations, perceiving that Titan's secrets stretch out past the expected.

The Titan Explorer turns into a stage for logical talk and request, with the group participating in cooperative conversations to decipher the information and pictures sent from the subsurface. The surprising difficulties and disclosures just strengthen the logical interest encompassing Titan's subsurface sea. Dr. Victoria Hayes, tending to the group at mission control, stresses the significance of keeping a receptive outlook and a feeling of request even with the unexplored world.

The Titan Explorer's excursion into Titan's subsurface sea unfurls as a powerful investigation, uncovering the known and obscure parts of Titan's extraordinary climate. The mechanical arms, controlled with accuracy by Dr. Alan Rodriguez and his group, become instruments of logical request, gathering tests and leading examinations that add to the developing assemblage of information about Titan's subsurface geography. The specific cameras, intended for organic investigation under the oversight of Dr. Marcus Thompson, catch pictures of Titan's submerged domain, giving a visual story of the extraterrestrial sea.

As the Titan Explorer proceeds with its investigation, the group faces the test of deciphering the information progressively and changing their speculations in light of the developing disclosures. The subsurface expanse of Titan, with its puzzling land developments and likely organic areas of interest, turns into a material for logical investigation. Dr. Emily Chang, working together with Dr. Alan Rodriguez and Dr. Marcus Thompson, drives the group in disentangling the complexities of Titan's subsurface climate.

The Titan Explorer's main goal, at first met with wariness, catches the consideration of established researchers and the more extensive public. The disclosures made, the difficulties survive, and the continuous investigation of Titan's sea add to a story that rises above the limits of planetary science. The group's devotion to thorough logical request, combined with their capacity to adjust to unanticipated conditions, accumulates regard and backing from their companions.

As the Titan Explorer proceeds with its plunge into the maritime profundities, the group at mission control thinks about the groundbreaking idea of the mission. The logical talk encompassing Titan's subsurface sea turns into a subject of worldwide interest, with scientists and space fans enthusiastically anticipating refreshes from the mission. Dr. Victoria Hayes, tending to the worldwide crowd, underlines the cooperative idea of logical investigation and welcomes mankind to partake in the fervor of unwinding the secrets that plague our nearby planet group.

4.3 Technical challenges and the team's resilience during the descent.

The plummet into Titan's subsurface sea presents the Titan Explorer group with a heap of specialized difficulties, pushing the limits of designing and logical investigation.

As the sub dives into the outsider climate of fluid hydrocarbons, the group faces unforeseen obstacles that require versatility, flexibility, and creative critical thinking. Dr. Victoria Hayes, driving the mission, directs the group through the complexities of extraterrestrial investigation, where each challenge turns into a chance for logical disclosure and mechanical headway.

The specialized difficulties start as the Titan Explorer advances from the investigation of Titan's surface to its drop into the subsurface sea. Dr. Hayden Carter, the designer answerable for the drive framework, screens the mind boggling elements of Titan's climate and fluid hydrocarbons. The drive framework, intended for the double usefulness of barometrical passage and sea-going investigation, must consistently adjust to the evolving conditions, guaranteeing a controlled plummet into the subsurface sea.

Commandant James Mitchell, directing the Titan Explorer through the difficulties of the plunge, works together with Dr. Hayden Carter to improve the sub's direction. The thick climate of Titan presents one of a kind difficulties, calling for continuous acclimations to explore through the differing layers. The drive framework, pushed by a progression of controlled explodes, answers Commandant Mitchell's orders, permitting the submarine to penetrate through the air layers and dive into Titan's puzzling subsurface sea.

The plunge is a fragile dance among innovation and the unexplored world. Dr. Sophia Ramirez, directing the correspondence framework, guarantees that the Titan Explorer keeps a steady connection with mission control. The transmission of information in the submerged climate of Titan's sea requests refined signal handling and correspondence conventions. Dr. Ramirez's skill becomes critical in keeping a solid association, permitting the group to get ongoing updates and go with informed choices during the drop.

As the Titan Explorer lowers into the fluid hydrocarbons, Dr. Alan Rodriguez assumes responsibility for the automated arms. The difficulties of exploring through an outsider sea floor, set apart by expected geographical developments and organic areas of interest, require exact control and versatility. Dr. Rodriguez and his group control the mechanical arms to collaborate with the sea depths, gather tests, and lead logical examinations — an accomplishment that requests a sensitive harmony among independence and human direction.

Dr. Marcus Thompson, directing the natural investigation, faces difficulties in deciphering the information from the particular cameras. The hydrocarbon-rich climate of Titan's sea presents one of a kind factors that influence the perceivability and translation of possible indications of something going on under the surface. Dr. Thompson works together with the imaging group to upgrade the capacities of the cameras, adapting to the particular states of Titan's subsurface. The quest for potential biosignatures turns into a specialized test that the group embraces with logical interest.

The surprising land developments on the sea depths represent a riddle for Dr. Emily Chang, the geologist on the mission. The Titan Explorer's plunge uncovers structures that overcome traditional presumption, inciting Dr. Chang and her group to reconsider how they might interpret Titan's land history. The subsurface climate, wealthy in hydrocarbons, adds layers of intricacy to the land examinations, requiring imaginative ways to deal with unravel the beginning and meaning of the found developments.

Dr. Victoria Hayes, driving the group with key vision, perceives the requirement for cooperative critical thinking. The specialized difficulties looked during the drop are not secluded obstructions but rather interconnected parts of a diverse mission.

Dr. Hayes cultivates a climate where interdisciplinary joint effort flourishes, permitting researchers and designers to pool their skill and address difficulties with an all encompassing point of view.

The group's flexibility becomes obvious as they experience surprising varieties in temperature and strain during the plunge. Dr. Hayden Carter's aptitude in warm control frameworks demonstrates instrumental in guaranteeing the Titan Explorer's usefulness under the outrageous states of Titan's subsurface. The sub's capacity to adjust to temperature changes while keeping up with functional respectability turns into a demonstration of the fastidious designing that supports the mission.

As the Titan Explorer proceeds with its plummet, the group faces the test of exploring through possibly risky locales of Titan's sea. Dr. Alan Rodriguez, collaborating with Leader James Mitchell, changes the sub's way to stay away from unexpected snags and guarantee the security of the mechanical arms. The fragile harmony among investigation and hazard moderation turns into a point of convergence, requiring consistent watchfulness and decision-production during the drop.

The particular cameras, intended for organic investigation, catch pictures of Titan's subsurface that challenge assumptions. Dr. Marcus Thompson's ability in sea life science becomes crucial as the group examines the recording for any indications of something going on under the surface or remarkable variations to Titan's hydrocarbon-rich climate. The specialized test of recognizing potential biosignatures turns into a co-operative undertaking, with researchers from different disciplines contributing their experiences.

The group's flexibility is tried further as the Titan Explorer experiences unidentified designs on the sea floor. Dr. Emily Chang, drawing on her land mastery, works together with Dr. Alan Rodriguez and the imaging group to investigate the information and pictures sent by the submarine. The surprising land developments brief the group to think about elective speculations regarding Titan's subsurface elements, testing assumptions and inciting a reconsideration of the mission's logical goals.

Dr. Victoria Hayes, tending to the group during a post-op interview meeting, recognizes the intricacies of the plummet and the unforeseen difficulties confronted. She underscores the significance of versatility and flexibility despite the obscure, empowering the group to see each test as a chance for disclosure. The mission, she notes, isn't exclusively about affirming existing speculations yet about embracing the vulnerability inborn in investigation.

· The specialized difficulties during the drop brief the group to carry out on-the-fly changes and upgrades. Dr. Sophia Ramirez, directing the correspondence framework, teams up with the designing group to improve the productivity of information transmission. The versatility of the correspondence framework becomes urgent in keeping a consistent progression of data, permitting the group to go with informed choices and adjust to the developing circumstances.

The startling disclosures on the sea floor, remembering bizarre varieties for temperature and unidentified designs, strengthen the logical talk inside the group. Dr. Emily

Chang, driving the topographical examinations, works together with Dr. Marcus Thompson and Dr. Alan Rodriguez to plan speculations and refine the mission's goals. The specialized difficulties become impetuses for logical request, pushing the limits of the's comprehension group might interpret Titan's subsurface climate.

As the Titan Explorer dives further into Titan's sea, the group experiences a unique climate that overcomes starting presumption. Dr. Hayden Carter, supervising the impetus framework, teams up with Commandant James Mitchell to streamline the sub's direction. The impetus framework, a wonder of designing inventiveness, adjusts to the developing circumstances, permitting the Titan Explorer to explore through the fluid hydrocarbons with accuracy.

The versatility of the group is additionally tried as the Titan Explorer faces unanticipated choppiness in Titan's sea. Dr. Victoria Hayes, depending on her essential initiative, directs the group through the difficulties, underlining the significance of information driven navigation. The group's capacity to investigate and adjust turns into a sign of the mission, exhibiting the flexibility fashioned through careful planning and a pledge to the quest for information.

Dr. Marcus Thompson, zeroing in on the natural investigation part, dissects the information from the specific cameras with elevated examination. The hydrocarbon-rich climate of Titan's sea, once thought to be cold, turns into a likely living space for novel types of life. The specialized test of deciphering the natural information turns into a cooperative exertion, with the group investigating the chance of uncovering extraterrestrial biosignatures.

The Titan Explorer's plummet, set apart by specialized difficulties and surprising disclosures, turns into a demonstration of human inventiveness and versatility. The group's capacity to adjust to the advancing circumstances, investigate unexpected issues, and proceed with the mission in spite of vulnerabilities highlights the soul of investigation that drives humankind's journey for information. Dr. Victoria Hayes, pondering the difficulties confronted, underlines that the mission's prosperity lies in the defeating of specialized obstacles as well as in the extraordinary effect on how we might interpret Titan's subsurface sea.

Chapter 5

Submersion into the Abyss

The submersion into the pit of Titan's subsurface sea addresses a peak in the Sub Stories Titan's Maritime Investigation, a perfection of careful preparation, mechanical development, and the aggregate endeavors of a different group of researchers, specialists, and wayfarers. Driven by the visionary Dr. Victoria Hayes, the Titan Explorer slides into the fluid hydrocarbons, wandering into the baffling profundities that have stayed covered underneath the moon's frigid hull.

As the Titan Explorer starts its plunge, Commandant James Mitchell assumes command over the submarine, directing it through the outsider climate of Titan's subsurface sea. The impetus framework, under the careful focus of Dr. Hayden Carter, draws in with accuracy, moving the sub further into the chasm. The group at mission control, including Dr. Sophia Ramirez supervising correspondence, intently screens the plunge, mindful that every second carries humankind closer to opening the insider facts of Titan's mysterious sea.

The plummet into the void is an excursion into the obscure, both deductively and innovatively. Dr. Emily Chang, the geologist, teams up with Leader Mitchell to decipher the geographical elements experienced during the plummet.

The Titan Explorer's sensors catch looks at the sea floor, uncovering interesting arrangements that challenge the group's predispositions about Titan's subsurface topography. Dr. Chang's geographical aptitude becomes instrumental in unraveling the ramifications of the advancing scene.

Dr. Alan Rodriguez, in charge of the automated arms, moves them with accuracy as the Titan Explorer moves toward the sea floor. The group faces the specialized test of guaranteeing that the automated arms can endure the tension and ecological states of Titan's pit. Dr. Rodriguez, drawing on his designing ability, organizes the sending of the mechanical arms to gather tests and lead logical investigations, transforming the chasm into a research facility for extraterrestrial investigation.

The Titan Explorer's drop turns into a tactile encounter as specific cameras catch the ethereal excellence of Titan's subsurface sea. Dr. Marcus Thompson, the sea life scientist administering the organic investigation, coordinates the cameras toward potential areas of interest that might hold onto indications of something going on under the surface. The hydrocarbon-rich climate, when thought cold, turns into a material for possible organic disclosures. The specialized difficulties of adjusting imaging frameworks to Titan's novel circumstances feature the group's capacity to develop on the fly.

As the Titan Explorer proceeds with its excursion into the pit, the group experiences surprising varieties in the structure and temperature of the fluid hydrocarbons. Dr. Emily Chang, teaming up with Dr. Alan Rodriguez, examines the information sent by the sub, endeavoring to unwind the secrets of Titan's subsurface climate. The specialized difficulties of deciphering the information continuously become a unique course of logical request, inciting the group to change their speculations and investigate the unexplored world.

The flexibility of the Titan Explorer group is apparent as the sub explores through the void, conquering specialized obstacles and unanticipated difficulties. Dr. Victoria Hayes, tending to the group at mission control, recognizes the intricacies of the plunge and stresses the authentic meaning of mankind's introduction to the profundities of an extraterrestrial sea. The chasm turns into a representative limit, denoting the progress from hypothesis to substantial investigation in the mission for grasping Titan's exceptional climate.

Dr. Sophia Ramirez's job in keeping up with correspondence turns out to be progressively significant as the Titan Explorer dives further into the chasm. The correspondence framework, exposed to the difficulties of Titan's subsurface, depends on cutting edge signal handling and transfer components to guarantee the nonstop progression of information. Dr. Ramirez's mastery in correspondence innovation becomes foremost as the group depends on a consistent stream of data to direct the Titan Explorer through the chasm.

The Titan Explorer's automated arms, controlled with accuracy by Dr. Alan Rodriguez and his group, gather tests from the sea floor. The geographical and possibly organic examples become a stash of information that holds the commitment of unwinding Titan's baffling secrets. Dr. Marcus Thompson, dissecting the natural information, examines the pictures for any indications of development or designs that might show the presence of life in Titan's void. The specialized difficulties of testing in an outsider climate highlight the creativity of the designing arrangements executed in the Titan Explorer.

The group's flexibility is tried further as the Titan Explorer experiences surprising varieties in the temperature and tension of the void. Dr. Hayden Carter, administering the drive framework, teams up with Leader James Mitchell to explore through locales of expected disturbance. The specialized difficulties of changing the submarine's way while keeping up with dependability become a powerful part of the plunge, featuring the flexibility of the designing arrangements executed in the Titan Explorer.

Dr. Victoria Hayes, with an essential vision, directs the group through the pit, underlining the significance of cooperation and interdisciplinary collaboration. The combination of logical aptitude with designing development turns into the foundation of the mission's prosperity. The pit, when a theoretical idea, changes into a substantial boondocks of investigation where mankind stands up to the difficulties of the enormous unexplored world.

The Titan Explorer's drop turns into a groundbreaking excursion for the group, both exclusively and by and large. The cooperative endeavors of researchers, designers, and travelers unite as the submarine arrives at more prominent profundities in Titan's chasm. Dr. Emily Chang's topographical investigations, Dr. Marcus Thompson's organic investigations, and Dr. Alan Rodriguez's mechanical controls synergize to make an extensive story of Titan's subsurface climate. The pit, when covered in secret, turns into a material for logical request and revelation.

As the Titan Explorer investigates the void, the group experiences startling topographical highlights on the sea floor. Dr. Emily Chang, drawing on her topographical skill, teams up with Dr. Alan Rodriguez to break down the information and pictures communicated by the submarine. The unforeseen geographical developments brief the group to reevaluate how they might interpret Titan's subsurface climate, stressing the powerful idea of extraterrestrial investigation.

The Titan Explorer's mechanical arms, controlled with accuracy by Dr. Alan Rodriguez and his group, become instruments of logical request, gathering tests and leading investigations that add to the developing assemblage of information about Titan's subsurface geography.

The particular cameras, intended for organic investigation under the oversight of Dr. Marcus Thompson, catch pictures of Titan's submerged domain, giving a visual story of the extraterrestrial sea. The void, when a riddle, turns into an embroidery of topographical marvels and likely organic secrets.

The Titan Explorer's central goal, at first met with wariness, catches the consideration of established researchers and the more extensive public. The revelations made, the difficulties survive, and the continuous investigation of Titan's pit add to a story that rises above the limits of planetary science. The group's commitment to thorough logical request, combined with their capacity to adjust to unanticipated conditions, collects regard and backing from their companions.

The submersion into the pit of Titan's subsurface sea turns into a groundbreaking second in the mission. Dr. Victoria Hayes, tending to the worldwide crowd, stresses the cooperative idea of logical investigation and welcomes humankind to partake in the fervor of disentangling the secrets that overrun our nearby planet group. The chasm, when a far off boondocks, turns into an image of mankind's unstoppable soul of investigation and the determined quest for information.

5.1 Titan Voyager reaches the surface of Titan's ocean.

The perfection of long stretches of arranging, mechanical advancement, and logical expectation, the second shows up as the Titan Explorer arrives at the outer layer of Titan's sea. Dr. Victoria Hayes, at the front of this spearheading mission, drives a group of researchers, designers, and pioneers who have resolutely pursued disentangling the secrets of Titan, Saturn's biggest moon. The surface investigation denotes a vital stage in Sub Stories Titan's Maritime Investigation, where the Titan Explorer rises up out of the void to explore the cold and cryptic territory of Titan's subsurface sea.

Leader James Mitchell, directing the Titan Explorer with accuracy, directs the submarine towards the outer layer of Titan's sea. The impetus framework, under the careful attention of Dr. Hayden Carter, connects with to guarantee a controlled rising. The group at mission control, including Dr. Sophia Ramirez regulating correspondence, screens the rising with a mix of energy and expectation. Each meter nearer to the surface is a stage towards uncovering the mysteries that have stayed secret underneath the cold covering of Titan.

As the Titan Explorer penetrates the outer layer of Titan's sea, the group observers an extraordinary second in the mission. Dr. Emily Chang, the geologist, teams up with Authority Mitchell to decipher the underlying pictures and information communicated by the submarine.

The surface elements come into center, uncovering a scene described by huge fields, transcending hills, and pools of fluid hydrocarbons. The land arrangements, molded by Titan's special natural circumstances, become the material for logical investigation.

Dr. Alan Rodriguez, answerable for the mechanical arms, directs their organization as the Titan Explorer floats over the surface. The mechanical arms, intended for accuracy and versatility, are prepared to cooperate with the territory, gather tests, and lead land examinations. Dr. Rodriguez and his group control the mechanical arms with a fragile touch, transforming the surface investigation into a logical expressive dance where every development adds to's how humankind might interpret Titan's geography.

The specific cameras, intended for organic investigation under the management of Dr. Marcus Thompson, catch high-goal pictures of Titan's surface. The hydrocarbon-rich lakes, when remembered to be ungracious, become likely natural surroundings for special types of life. Dr. Thompson examines the recording for indications of development or designs that might show the presence of life in this outsider climate. The specialized difficulties of imaging in Titan's environmental circumstances add an additional layer of intricacy to the organic investigation.

The Titan Explorer's development onto the surface turns into a festival of human inventiveness and investigation. Dr. Victoria Hayes, tending to the group, recognizes the noteworthy meaning of arriving at Titan's sea surface. The logical talk encompassing Titan's true capacity for extraterrestrial life and remarkable geographical arrangements is at this point not hypothetical — it is unfurling continuously as the submarine investigates the unfamiliar domains of Titan's subsurface sea.

The Titan Explorer's drive framework, finely tuned for the intricacies of Titan's climate, permits Administrator Mitchell to explore the submarine across the surface with accuracy. Dr. Hayden Carter's ability in drive elements guarantees that the Titan Explorer can navigate the different scene of Titan's sea, from the far reaching fields to the unpredictable ridge developments. The specialized difficulties of surface route become a demonstration of the designing arrangements that empower humankind to investigate the most distant spans of our nearby planet group.

Dr. Sophia Ramirez's job in keeping up with correspondence becomes essential as the Titan Explorer meanders the surface. The correspondence framework, exposed to Titan's climatic circumstances, depends on cutting edge signal handling to guarantee the consistent trade of information between the submarine and mission control. Dr. Ramirez's mastery in correspondence innovation guarantees that the group stays associated, considering ongoing decision-production during the surface investigation.

The Titan Explorer's mechanical arms, under the direction of Dr. Alan Rodriguez, connect with the surface landscape, gathering tests that hold the way to unwinding Titan's geographical history.

The group teams up to decipher the information continuously, changing their speculations in light of the developing disclosures. Dr. Emily Chang's topographical examinations become instrumental in translating the meaning of the surface highlights, giving experiences into the cycles that have formed Titan's scene after some time.

Dr. Marcus Thompson, zeroing in on the natural investigation, examines the pictures caught by the specific cameras for any indications of something going on under the surface or extraordinary transformations. The Titan Explorer's capacity to catch high-goal pictures in Titan's environmental circumstances turns into a mechanical victory, opening new roads for the investigation of potential biosignatures. The surface investigation becomes a geographical excursion as well as a journey for figuring out the expected tenability of Titan's hydrocarbon-rich climate.

As the Titan Explorer crosses Titan's sea surface, startling geographical highlights catch the group's consideration. Dr. Emily Chang, drawing on her topographical aptitude, works together with Dr. Alan Rodriguez and the imaging group to break down the information and pictures sent by the sub. The startling land arrangements brief the group to reconsider how they might interpret Titan's surface elements, featuring the dynamic and steadily changing nature of extraterrestrial investigation.

The Titan Explorer's excursion across the surface turns into a powerful investigation, with the group adjusting to the developing circumstances and settling on continuous choices to boost logical experiences. Dr. Victoria Hayes, tending to the group at mission control, stresses the significance of staying receptive and lithe notwithstanding the unexplored world. The surface investigation turns into a demonstration of the group's capacity to explore the intricacies of Titan's current circumstance and change difficulties into valuable open doors for disclosure.

The Titan Explorer's presence on Titan's sea surface catches the creative mind of the worldwide local area. The pictures and information communicated from the sub become a wellspring of motivation, welcoming individuals all over the planet to partake in the fervor of extraterrestrial investigation. Dr. Victoria Hayes, recognizing the worldwide crowd, underlines the cooperative idea of logical revelation and urges humankind to embrace the soul of investigation that rises above public limits.

The Titan Explorer's surface investigation turns into a spearheading section in the continuous adventure of Sub Stories Titan's Maritime Investigation. The group's capacity to arrive at the surface, gather tests, and direct land and organic investigations hoists the mission higher than ever of logical accomplishment. Dr. Victoria Hayes, tending to the worldwide crowd, thinks about the extraordinary idea of the mission and welcomes humankind to proceed with the excursion of investigation and illumination in the vast expanse of conceivable outcomes.

5.2 Initial discoveries and challenges as the submersible begins its descent into the abyss.

As the Titan Explorer leaves on its plummet into the pit of Titan's subsurface sea, the underlying disclosures and difficulties unfurl, making way for an excursion of phenomenal investigation and logical request. Dr. Victoria Hayes, driving a group of specialists in different fields, directs the submarine through the outsider climate of fluid hydrocarbons, where every second turns into a gateway to the unexplored world.

Leader James Mitchell, in charge of the Titan Explorer, teams up with Dr. Hayden Carter, supervising the impetus framework, to start the controlled plunge. The impetus framework, fastidiously intended for the double usefulness of air section and seagoing investigation, draws in with accuracy. The group at mission control, including Dr. Sophia Ramirez overseeing correspondence, intently screens the underlying phases of the drop, mindful that this stage denotes the progress from surface investigation to the baffling profundities of Titan's subsurface sea.

The primary snapshots of plummet uncover the difficulties of exploring through Titan's thick climate. Commandant Mitchell, attracting on his skill heavenly route, changes the direction to improve the sub's way. Dr. Hayden Carter's job becomes significant as the impetus framework adjusts to the changing environmental circumstances, guaranteeing a smooth progress from the surface to the profundities beneath.

Dr. Emily Chang, the geologist on the mission, teams up with Leader Mitchell to decipher the land highlights experienced during the underlying plunge. The Titan Explorer's sensors catch pictures of the sea depths, divulging interesting arrangements that challenge the group's biases about Titan's subsurface geography. Dr. Chang's topographical skill becomes instrumental in translating the ramifications of the developing scene, transforming each geographical disclosure into a piece of the riddle that might open the mysteries of Titan's land development.

As the Titan Explorer proceeds with its plummet, Dr. Alan Rodriguez assumes responsibility for the automated arms, intended for accuracy and flexibility in the difficult climate of Titan's chasm. The group faces the specialized test of guaranteeing that the automated arms can endure the strain and ecological states of the subsurface sea. Dr. Rodriguez organizes the sending of the mechanical arms to gather tests from the sea floor, transforming the chasm into a lab for extraterrestrial investigation.

Dr. Marcus Thompson, regulating the organic investigation, examines the underlying pictures caught by the particular cameras. The hydrocarbon-rich climate of

Titan's sea presents remarkable factors that influence the perceivability and translation of expected indications of something going on under the surface.

Dr. Thompson works together with the imaging group to upgrade the capacities of the cameras, adapting to the particular states of Titan's subsurface. The quest for potential biosignatures turns into a specialized test that the group embraces with logical interest.

The Titan Explorer's plunge turns into a unique investigation, with each layer of the subsurface uncovering new secrets. Unidentified designs on the sea floor, strange varieties in temperature, and puzzling land developments brief the group to rethink how they might interpret Titan's subsurface climate. Dr. Chang, drawing on her land skill, drives the group in unraveling the ramifications of these disclosures, perceiving that Titan's secrets stretch out past the expected.

Dr. Victoria Hayes, tending to the group at mission control, recognizes the underlying disclosures and difficulties looked during the plunge. She underscores the significance of flexibility and cooperation even with the obscure, establishing the vibe for a mission that embraces vulnerability as an essential piece of logical investigation.

The Titan Explorer's excursion into the void turns into a stage for logical talk and request. The surprising difficulties and revelations just heighten the logical interest encompassing Titan's subsurface sea. Dr. Hayes urges the group to keep a receptive outlook and a feeling of request, stressing that the mission's prosperity lies in affirming existing speculations as well as in embracing the groundbreaking capability of startling discoveries.

As the Titan Explorer digs further into the subsurface sea, the group experiences varieties in temperature and tension that were not completely expected. Dr. Hayden Carter's skill in warm control frameworks demonstrates instrumental in guaranteeing the Titan Explorer's usefulness under the outrageous states of Titan's pit. The sub's capacity to adjust to temperature variances while keeping up with functional respectability turns into a demonstration of the careful designing that supports the mission.

The particular cameras, intended for natural investigation, catch pictures of Titan's subsurface that challenge assumptions. Dr. Marcus Thompson's aptitude in sea life science becomes significant as the group examines the recording for any indications of something going on under the surface or novel variations to Titan's hydrocarbon-rich climate. The specialized test of recognizing potential biosignatures turns into a cooperative undertaking, with researchers from different disciplines contributing their experiences.

The group's versatility becomes obvious as the Titan Explorer experiences unidentified designs on the sea depths. Dr. Emily Chang, drawing on her topographical skill, teams up with Dr. Alan Rodriguez and the imaging group to break down the information and pictures sent by the sub. The unforeseen land developments brief the group to think about elective speculations regarding Titan's subsurface elements, testing assumptions and provoking a reexamination of the mission's logical targets.

Dr. Victoria Hayes, tending to the group during a post-op interview meeting, recognizes the intricacies of the plummet and the surprising difficulties confronted. She underscores the significance of flexibility and versatility even with the obscure, empowering the group to see each test as a chance for disclosure. The mission, she notes, isn't exclusively about affirming existing speculations however about embracing the vulnerability inborn in investigation.

The specialized difficulties during the plunge brief the group to carry out on-the-fly changes and enhancements. Dr. Sophia Ramirez, regulating the correspondence framework, teams up with the designing group to improve the productivity of information transmission. The flexibility of the correspondence framework becomes pivotal in keeping a consistent progression of data, permitting the group to go with informed choices and adjust to the developing circumstances.

The startling revelations on the sea floor, remembering bizarre varieties for temperature and unidentified designs, increase the logical talk inside the group. Dr. Emily Chang, driving the topographical investigations, teams up with Dr. Marcus Thompson and Dr. Alan Rodriguez to plan speculations and refine the mission's targets. The specialized difficulties become impetuses for logical request, pushing the limits of the's comprehension group might interpret Titan's subsurface climate.

As the Titan Explorer dives further into Titan's sea, the group experiences a unique climate that overcomes starting presumption. Dr. Hayden Carter, regulating the drive framework, teams up with Leader James Mitchell to streamline the submarine's direction. The impetus framework, a wonder of designing inventiveness, adjusts to the developing circumstances, permitting the Titan Explorer to explore through the fluid hydrocarbons with accuracy.

The strength of the group is additionally tried as the Titan Explorer faces unexpected disturbance in Titan's sea. Dr. Victoria Hayes, depending on her essential authority, directs the group through the difficulties, underscoring the significance of information driven navigation. The group's capacity to investigate and adjust turns into a sign of the mission, showing the strength fashioned through careful readiness and a pledge to the quest for information.

Dr. Marcus Thompson, zeroing in on the natural investigation part, breaks down the information from the specific cameras with uplifted examination. The hydrocarbon-rich climate of Titan's sea, once thought to be unwelcoming, turns into a likely living space for novel types of life. The specialized test of deciphering the natural information turns into a cooperative exertion, with the group investigating the chance of uncovering extraterrestrial biosignatures.

The Titan Explorer's drop, set apart by specialized difficulties and surprising revelations, turns into a demonstration of human inventiveness and versatility.

The group's capacity to adjust to the advancing circumstances, investigate unexpected issues, and proceed with the mission notwithstanding vulnerabilities highlights the soul of investigation that drives humankind's journey for information. Dr. Victoria Hayes, thinking about the difficulties confronted, underscores that the mission's prosperity lies in the defeating of specialized obstacles as well as in the extraordinary effect on how we might interpret Titan's subsurface sea.

5.3 Encounter with unique and unexpected life forms in Titan's dark waters.

As the Titan Explorer proceeds with its plummet into the dim waters of Titan's subsurface sea, the mission takes a remarkable turn with the startling experience with one of a kind and mysterious living things. Dr. Victoria Hayes, driving the assorted group of researchers, designers, and adventurers, guides the sub into unfamiliar regions where the secrets of Titan's secret sea show some signs of life.

Authority James Mitchell, at the controls of the Titan Explorer, teams up with Dr. Hayden Carter, regulating the impetus framework, to explore through the dim and puzzling profundities. The drive framework, intended for flexibility in Titan's outsider climate, answers Commandant Mitchell's orders as the submarine dives further into the sea's pit. The group at mission control, including Dr. Sophia Ramirez overseeing correspondence, expects every second with a mix of fervor and logical interest.

The primary signs of remarkable living things arise on the Titan Explorer's specific cameras, catching the consideration of Dr. Marcus Thompson, directing the natural investigation. The hydrocarbon-rich climate, once thought to be ungracious, turns into a possible territory for creatures that overcome customary presumption. Dr. Thompson and the imaging group examine the recording, looking for indications of development, particular designs, or any signs of life in Titan's dim waters.

Dr. Alan Rodriguez, answerable for the automated arms, changes their developments with accuracy as the Titan Explorer moves toward the charming living things. The group faces the test of collaborating with these obscure life forms, gathering tests, and directing logical investigations. Dr. Rodriguez's aptitude becomes vital as the automated arms gently move to try not to upset the recently discovered life structures while social occasion important information for additional review.

The experience with startling living things prompts Dr. Emily Chang, the geologist, to reevaluate the geographical setting of the sea floor. The presence of creatures might show a powerful transaction among topography and science in Titan's subsurface climate.

Dr. Chang works together with Dr. Marcus Thompson, Dr. Alan Rodriguez, and Commandant James Mitchell to incorporate the geographical and natural information, winding around an exhaustive story of Titan's special biological system.

Dr. Victoria Hayes, tending to the group during the experience, accentuates the notable idea of the revelation and the requirement for fastidious documentation and investigation. The group's logical instruments become instruments of disclosure, catching information that could reshape's comprehension humankind might interpret extraterrestrial life and the possible livability of far off universes.

As the Titan Explorer drifts close to the living things, the specific cameras give definite pictures that uncover the multifaceted highlights of these creatures. Dr. Marcus Thompson, with his experience in sea life science, perceives examples and ways of behaving that allude to the transformation systems created because of Titan's particular natural circumstances. The specialized difficulties of catching clear pictures in obscurity waters become wins as the group acquires exceptional experiences into Titan's subsurface biological system.

Dr. Sophia Ramirez, regulating the correspondence framework, guarantees that the experience is communicated progressively to mission control and, thusly, to a world-wide crowd. The surprising disclosure catches the creative mind of researchers, space lovers, and the more extensive public, encouraging a feeling of aggregate marvel and interest in the conceivable outcomes that lie past Earth.

The Titan Explorer's automated arms, controlled with accuracy by Dr. Alan Rodriguez and his group, delicately gather tests from the area of the living things. The test of test assortment turns into a sensitive dance between logical request and conservation of the freshly discovered organic entities. Dr. Rodriguez guarantees that the mechanical arms agree with rigid conventions to limit aggravation and keep up with the trustworthiness of the examples.

The logical talk inside the group increases as the experience with extraordinary living things opens up new roads of request. Dr. Emily Chang, drawing on her land mastery, works together with Dr. Marcus Thompson to comprehend the land setting of the existence structures' environment. The unforeseen beneficial interaction among geography and science challenges assumptions about Titan's subsurface climate, pro-voking the group to reevaluate the interconnectedness of planetary cycles.

The Titan Explorer's process through Titan's dull waters turns into an entrancing dance among investigation and logical request. The group's flexibility and versatility sparkle as they explore through the startling experience with living things, changing their way to deal with expand the logical yield while limiting impedance with the freshly discovered organic entities. Dr. Victoria Hayes compliments the group's co-operative endeavors, featuring the significance of interdisciplinary collaboration not-withstanding such earth shattering disclosures.

Dr. Marcus Thompson, breaking down the organic information, starts to figure out speculations about the idea of the living things and their likely transformations. The hydrocarbon-rich climate, portrayed by low temperatures and one of a kind en-vironmental circumstances, challenges ordinary suppositions about the prerequisites forever. Dr. Thompson's aptitude becomes vital as the group tries to comprehend the complexities of Titan's dim waters and the biological specialties involved by these startling organic entities.

As the Titan Explorer proceeds with its investigation, the group experiences extra pockets of remarkable living things, each introducing another arrangement of diffi-culties and potential open doors for logical disclosure. Dr. Alan Rodriguez, regulating the mechanical arms, adjusts their developments to represent varieties in the landscape and the way of behaving of the organic entities. The group teams up progressively to refine their methodology, guaranteeing that the experience yields a rich stash of information for resulting investigation.

The Titan Explorer's experience with surprising living things turns into a guide of motivation for the more extensive academic local area and general society. Dr. Victoria Hayes, tending to a worldwide crowd, underlines the cooperative idea of logical investigation and the extraordinary effect of startling revelations. The experience with living things in Titan's dim waters turns into a demonstration of humankind's capacity to adjust, enhance, and investigate the secrets of the universe.

The logical examinations of the gathered examples, led with accuracy by the group on board the Titan Explorer, uncover the biochemical marks of the living things. Dr. Marcus Thompson's aptitude in science becomes vital as the group tries to comprehend the metabolic cycles and potential transformations that empower these organic entities to flourish in Titan's exceptional climate. The startling idea of the experience adds an additional layer of energy to the logical request, inciting the group to refine their speculations and push the limits of astrobiology.

Dr. Emily Chang, with her geographical foundation, teams up with Dr. Hayden Carter to coordinate the geographical setting of the experience into the more extensive comprehension of Titan's subsurface. The interaction among geography and science turns into a point of convergence of request, testing customary ideal models and provoking the group to investigate the interconnected elements that shape Titan's maritime biological system.

The Titan Explorer's experience with startling living things turns into a pivotal occasion in Submarine Stories Titan's Maritime Investigation. Dr. Victoria Hayes, thinking about the noteworthy meaning of the disclosure, highlights the mission's effect on how we might interpret the likely livability of divine bodies past Earth. The unforeseen living things in Titan's dim waters become representatives of the grandiose variety that anticipates investigation in the profundities of our planetary group and then some.

Chapter 6

Unveiling Titan's Secrets

As the Titan Explorer digs further into the pit of Titan's subsurface sea, the mission arrives at a crucial stage: the disclosing of Titan's insider facts. Dr. Victoria Hayes, at the very front of this pivotal investigation, drives a different group of researchers, specialists, and pioneers anxious to disentangle the secrets covered underneath the frosty hull of Saturn's biggest moon.

Administrator James Mitchell, directing the Titan Explorer with accuracy, teams up with Dr. Hayden Carter, directing the impetus framework, to explore through the perplexing climate of Titan's subsurface sea. The impetus framework, intended for flexibility in Titan's outsider circumstances, answers Commandant Mitchell's orders as the submarine plunges further into the chasm. The group at mission control, including Dr. Sophia Ramirez overseeing correspondence, expects the unfurling revelations with a mix of fervor and logical expectation.

The primary looks at the sea depths uncover a scene not at all like anything seen previously. Dr. Emily Chang, the geologist, teams up with Commandant Mitchell to decipher the geographical highlights experienced during the plummet.

The Titan Explorer's sensors catch high-goal pictures, uncovering interesting arrangements that challenge the group's assumptions about Titan's subsurface topography. Dr. Chang's topographical skill becomes instrumental in translating the ramifications of the developing scene, transforming every revelation into a piece of the riddle that might open the mysteries of Titan's geographical history.

As the Titan Explorer explores the sea depths, Dr. Alan Rodriguez assumes command over the mechanical arms, intended for accuracy and versatility in Titan's difficult climate. The group faces the specialized test of gathering tests and leading logical examinations of the sea depths. Dr. Rodriguez coordinates the organization of the mechanical arms, transforming the pit into a lab for extraterrestrial investigation. The examples accumulated become windows into Titan's geographical creation, giving important experiences into the cycles molding the moon's subsurface.

Dr. Marcus Thompson, supervising the natural investigation, coordinates the particular cameras towards potential areas of interest that might hold onto indications of something going on under the surface. The hydrocarbon-rich climate, once thought to be unwelcoming, turns into a material for expected natural revelations. Dr. Thompson examines the pictures for any indications of development or designs that might show the presence of life in Titan's pit. The specialized difficulties of imaging in Titan's climatic circumstances add an additional layer of intricacy to the natural investigation.

The Titan Explorer's excursion through the chasm turns into a tangible encounter as the specific cameras catch the ethereal excellence of Titan's subsurface sea. Dr. Marcus Thompson, examining the natural information, teams up with Dr. Alan Rodriguez and Dr. Emily Chang to associate the natural discoveries with the geographical elements. The interaction among science and geography turns into a point of convergence of request, provoking the group to investigate the expected associations between Titan's subsurface cycles and the presence of life.

Startling varieties in the organization and temperature of the fluid hydrocarbons challenge the group as they investigate further into the chasm. Dr. Hayden Carter, directing the impetus framework, teams up with Administrator James Mitchell to explore through locales of likely choppiness. The specialized difficulties of changing the sub's way while keeping up with security become a unique part of the drop, featuring the flexibility of the designing arrangements carried out in the Titan Explorer.

Dr. Victoria Hayes, tending to the group at mission control, recognizes the intricacies of the drop and the surprising difficulties confronted. She underscores the authentic meaning of humankind's introduction to the profundities of an extraterrestrial sea and the significance of constancy notwithstanding vulnerability.

The revealing of Titan's mysteries turns into an aggregate undertaking, with each colleague contributing their mastery to decipher the messages concealed in the moon's subsurface.

As the Titan Explorer proceeds with its investigation, the group experiences unforeseen land highlights on the sea floor. Dr. Emily Chang, drawing on her geographical mastery, works together with Dr. Alan Rodriguez and the imaging group to investigate the information and pictures communicated by the sub. The unforeseen geographical developments brief the group to reevaluate how they might interpret Titan's subsurface climate, stressing the unique idea of extraterrestrial investigation.

The Titan Explorer's mechanical arms, controlled with accuracy by Dr. Alan Rodriguez and his group, become instruments of logical request, gathering tests and leading investigations that add to the developing collection of information about Titan's subsurface geography. The specific cameras, intended for natural investigation under the oversight of Dr. Marcus Thompson, catch pictures of Titan's submerged domain, giving a visual story of the extraterrestrial sea. The chasm, when a conundrum, turns into an embroidery of topographical miracles and possible organic secrets.

As the Titan Explorer investigates the void, the group experiences unforeseen topographical highlights on the sea depths. Dr. Emily Chang, drawing on her topographical aptitude, teams up with Dr. Alan Rodriguez and the imaging group to break down the information and pictures sent by the submarine. The startling land arrangements brief the group to reconsider how they might interpret Titan's subsurface climate, accentuating the unique idea of extraterrestrial investigation.

The Titan Explorer's mechanical arms, controlled with accuracy by Dr. Alan Rodriguez and his group, become instruments of logical request, gathering tests and leading examinations that add to the developing assemblage of information about Titan's subsurface geography. The specific cameras, intended for organic investigation under the management of Dr. Marcus Thompson, catch pictures of Titan's submerged domain, giving a visual story of the extraterrestrial sea. The pit, when a mystery, turns into an embroidery of land miracles and possible natural secrets.

As the Titan Explorer investigates the pit, the group experiences unforeseen varieties in the sythesis and temperature of the fluid hydrocarbons. Dr. Emily Chang, working together with Dr. Alan Rodriguez, breaks down the information communicated by the submarine, endeavoring to disentangle the secrets of Titan's subsurface climate. The specialized difficulties of deciphering the information progressively become a unique course of logical request, inciting the group to change their speculations and investigate the unexplored world.

The flexibility of the Titan Explorer group is clear as the sub explores through the void, beating specialized obstacles and unanticipated difficulties. Dr. Victoria Hayes, tending to the group at mission control, recognizes the intricacies of the plummet and the unforeseen revelations made. She highlights the significance of versatility and coordinated effort, underlining that the mission's prosperity lies in affirming existing speculations as well as in embracing the groundbreaking capability of startling discoveries.

The experience with unforeseen land developments and varieties in the organization of the fluid hydrocarbons adds layers of intricacy to the logical talk inside the group. Dr. Emily Chang, Dr. Alan Rodriguez, and Dr. Hayden Carter team up to translate the ramifications of these revelations, perceiving that Titan's subsurface is a dynamic and developing climate. The chasm, when seen as a static domain, turns into a demonstration of the unique interchange of geographical cycles inside an extraterrestrial sea.

The Titan Explorer's drop into the void turns into an excursion of divulging Titan's mysteries, with every revelation testing assumptions and extending the skylines of human information. The geographical marvels and surprising varieties in the arrangement of Titan's subsurface sea become basic parts of the advancing account. Dr. Victoria Hayes, driving the group with vital vision, energizes the soul of investigation and interest that characterizes mankind's mission for grasping the secrets of the universe.

The Titan Explorer's plummet into the chasm turns into a critical part in Submarine Stories Titan's Maritime Investigation. The group's capacity to adjust to the unique climate of Titan's subsurface, conquer specialized difficulties, and make noteworthy disclosures highlights the versatility and assurance that drive logical investigation. Dr. Victoria Hayes, considering the excursion, welcomes mankind to partake in the energy of disclosing Titan's mysteries and to embrace the continuous experience of investigating the grandiose unexplored world.

6.1 Exploration of Titan's underwater landscape and geological features.

The investigation of Titan's submerged scene denotes a noteworthy part in the Submarine Stories Titan's Maritime Investigation, with the Titan Explorer exploring through the profundities of an extraterrestrial sea. Dr. Victoria Hayes, in charge of the mission, drives a group of researchers, specialists, and wayfarers on a journey to unwind the geographical secrets concealed underneath the cold outside of Saturn's biggest moon.

Administrator James Mitchell, controlling the Titan Explorer with accuracy, works together with Dr. Hayden Carter, directing the impetus framework, to navigate the submerged scene. The drive framework, adjusted for versatility in Titan's special climate, answers Leader Mitchell's orders as the submarine dives further into the sea's pit.

The group at mission control, including Dr. Sophia Ramirez overseeing correspondence, screens the investigation with a feeling of expectation as Titan's privileged insights unfurl.

The principal topographical elements come into center as the Titan Explorer's sensors catch high-goal pictures of the submerged landscape. Dr. Emily Chang, the geologist, teams up with Authority Mitchell to decipher the land arrangements experienced during the plummet. Transcending submerged mountains, huge fields, and multifaceted valleys shape the extraterrestrial scene, testing the group's assumptions about Titan's subsurface topography. Dr. Chang's land mastery becomes instrumental in translating the ramifications of the developing territory, transforming every revelation into a geographical unique piece.

As the Titan Explorer proceeds with its investigation, Dr. Alan Rodriguez assumes control over the automated arms, intended for accuracy and versatility in the difficult climate of Titan's submerged domain. The group faces the specialized test of interfacing with the submerged scene, gathering tests, and leading topographical examinations. Dr. Rodriguez organizes the sending of the mechanical arms, transforming the pit into a logical research facility for extraterrestrial investigation. The examples gathered give experiences into the topographical arrangement of Titan's subsurface, opening the mysteries of the moon's set of experiences written in its rough landscape.

Dr. Marcus Thompson, administering the natural investigation, coordinates the particular cameras towards potential environments that might hold onto indications of something going on under the surface. The hydrocarbon-rich climate, once viewed as cold, turns into a material for possible organic disclosures. Dr. Thompson examines the pictures for any indications of development or designs that might demonstrate the presence of life in Titan's submerged scene. The specialized difficulties of imaging in

Titan's barometrical circumstances add an additional layer of intricacy to the organic investigation.

The Titan Explorer's process through Titan's submerged scene turns into a visual banquet as the specific cameras catch the extraordinary excellence of the extraterrestrial sea. Dr. Marcus Thompson, examining the natural information, teams up with Dr. Alan Rodriguez and Dr. Emily Chang to associate the natural discoveries with the geographical elements. The interaction among science and geography turns into a point of convergence of request, inciting the group to investigate the possible associations between Titan's subsurface cycles and the presence of life.

Unforeseen varieties in the submerged landscape present difficulties and open doors for the group. Dr. Hayden Carter, directing the impetus framework, teams up with Authority James Mitchell to explore through districts of possible disturbance and unfamiliar geographical highlights.

The specialized difficulties of changing the sub's way while keeping up with dependability become a unique part of the investigation, exhibiting the versatility of the designing arrangements carried out in the Titan Explorer.

Dr. Victoria Hayes, tending to the group at mission control, recognizes the intricacies of investigating Titan's submerged scene and the unexpected difficulties confronted. She highlights the verifiable meaning of mankind's investigation underneath the outer layer of an extraterrestrial sea and the significance of versatility even with vulnerability. The investigation turns into a demonstration of human resourcefulness and versatility, pushing the limits of how we might interpret the universe.

The experience with unforeseen geographical arrangements and varieties in the submerged territory adds layers of intricacy to the logical talk inside the group. Dr. Emily Chang, Dr. Alan Rodriguez, and Dr. Hayden Carter team up to translate the ramifications of these disclosures, perceiving that Titan's submerged scene is a dynamic and developing climate. The pit, when seen as a static domain, turns into a demonstration of the unique interchange of geographical cycles inside an extraterrestrial sea.

The Titan Explorer's automated arms, controlled with accuracy by Dr. Alan Rodriguez and his group, become instruments of logical request, gathering tests and directing investigations that add to the developing collection of information about Titan's subsurface geography. The specific cameras, intended for organic investigation under the oversight of Dr. Marcus Thompson, catch pictures of Titan's submerged domain, giving a visual story of the extraterrestrial sea. The pit, when a conundrum, turns into an embroidery of topographical miracles and likely organic secrets.

As the Titan Explorer investigates the submerged scene, the group experiences surprising land highlights on the sea floor. Dr. Emily Chang, drawing on her topographical skill, works together with Dr. Alan Rodriguez and the imaging group to break down the information and pictures communicated by the sub. The startling land developments brief the group to rethink how they might interpret Titan's subsurface climate, underscoring the powerful idea of extraterrestrial investigation.

The Titan Explorer's mechanical arms, controlled with accuracy by Dr. Alan

Rodriguez and his group, become instruments of logical request, gathering tests and leading examinations that add to the developing collection of information about Titan's subsurface geography. The specific cameras, intended for natural investigation under the oversight of Dr. Marcus Thompson, catch pictures of Titan's submerged domain, giving a visual story of the extraterrestrial sea. The chasm, when a puzzle, turns into an embroidery of land miracles and expected natural secrets.

As the Titan Explorer investigates the chasm, the group experiences unforeseen varieties in the organization and temperature of the fluid hydrocarbons. Dr. Emily Chang, working together with Dr. Alan Rodriguez, dissects the information communicated by the submarine, endeavoring to unwind the secrets of Titan's subsurface climate. The specialized difficulties of deciphering the information progressively become a powerful course of logical request, inciting the group to change their speculations and investigate the unexplored world.

The flexibility of the Titan Explorer group is obvious as the sub explores through the chasm, conquering specialized obstacles and unanticipated difficulties. Dr. Victoria Hayes, tending to the group at mission control, recognizes the intricacies of the drop and the surprising revelations made. She highlights the significance of versatility and coordinated effort, underscoring that the mission's prosperity lies in affirming existing speculations as well as in embracing the extraordinary capability of surprising discoveries.

The experience with startling geographical developments and varieties in the sythesis of the fluid hydrocarbons adds layers of intricacy to the logical talk inside the group. Dr. Emily Chang, Dr. Alan Rodriguez, and Dr. Hayden Carter team up to unravel the ramifications of these disclosures, perceiving that Titan's submerged scene is a dynamic and developing climate. The chasm, when seen as a static domain, turns into a demonstration of the unique interaction of geographical cycles inside an extra-terrestrial sea.

The Titan Explorer's drop into the void turns into an excursion of revealing Titan's mysteries, with every revelation testing assumptions and extending the skylines of human information. The land ponders and unforeseen varieties in the sythesis of Titan's subsurface sea become basic parts of the developing story. Dr. Victoria Hayes, driving the group with vital vision, energizes the soul of investigation and interest that characterizes humankind's journey for grasping the secrets of the universe.

The Titan Explorer's plunge into the pit turns into a urgent part in Submarine Stories Titan's Maritime Investigation. The group's capacity to adjust to the powerful climate of Titan's subsurface, beat specialized difficulties, and make noteworthy disclosures highlights the strength and assurance that drive logical investigation. Dr. Victoria Hayes, pondering the excursion, welcomes humankind to partake in the fervor of uncovering Titan's mysteries and to embrace the continuous experience of investigating the astronomical unexplored world.

6.2 The team uncovers clues about the moon's history and evolution.

As the Titan Explorer dives into the secrets of Titan's subsurface sea, the group sets out on an excursion of logical request, uncovering significant pieces of information about the moon's set of experiences and development. Dr. Victoria Hayes, driving the undertaking, directs a group of interdisciplinary specialists in unwinding the mysteries hid underneath the frosty outside layer of Saturn's biggest moon.

Officer James Mitchell, guiding the Titan Explorer with accuracy, teams up with Dr. Hayden Carter, managing the drive framework, to explore through the moon's perplexing subsurface. The impetus framework, a wonder of designing flexibility, answers Leader Mitchell's orders as the submarine outlines its course through Titan's secret sea. The group at mission control, including Dr. Sophia Ramirez overseeing correspondence, anticipates every disclosure with a blend of fervor and logical interest.

The principal indications of land highlights on the sea floor enamor Dr. Emily Chang, the geologist, who teams up with Authority Mitchell to decipher the developing scene. High-goal pictures caught by the Titan Explorer's sensors uncover an intricate embroidery of edges, valleys, and geographical developments, proposing a powerful history for Titan's subsurface. Dr. Chang's land skill becomes instrumental in sorting out the riddle of Titan's topographical development, with every development recounting an account of the moon's past.

As the Titan Explorer proceeds with its investigation, Dr. Alan Rodriguez assumes responsibility for the mechanical arms, finely tuned for accuracy in Titan's difficult climate. The group faces the specialized test of gathering tests from the sea depths, leading land investigations that guarantee to uncover Titan's geographical mysteries. Dr. Rodriguez organizes the sending of the mechanical arms, transforming the pit into a logical research center for the fastidious assessment of Titan's subsurface organization.

Dr. Marcus Thompson, administering the organic investigation, coordinates the specific cameras towards potential areas of interest that might hold onto indications of something going on under the surface. The hydrocarbon-rich climate, once viewed as unfriendly, turns into a material for expected natural disclosures. Dr. Thompson examines the pictures for any indications of development or designs that might demonstrate the presence of life in Titan's subsurface sea. The specialized difficulties of imaging in Titan's climatic circumstances add an additional layer of intricacy to the natural investigation.

The Titan Explorer's process through Titan's subsurface sea turns into a visual banquet as the particular cameras catch the supernatural excellence of the extraterrestrial domain. Dr. Marcus Thompson, examining the natural information, works together with Dr. Alan Rodriguez and Dr. Emily Chang to associate the natural discoveries with the land highlights. The interaction among science and geography turns into a point of convergence of request, provoking the group to investigate the possible associations between Titan's subsurface cycles and the presence of life.

Surprising varieties in the piece and design of the sea floor present difficulties and open doors for the group. Dr. Hayden Carter, directing the impetus framework, teams up with Leader James Mitchell to explore through districts of likely disturbance and unfamiliar land highlights.

The specialized difficulties of changing the submarine's way while keeping up with solidness become a powerful part of the investigation, exhibiting the flexibility of the designing arrangements carried out in the Titan Explorer.

Dr. Victoria Hayes, tending to the group at mission control, recognizes the intricacies of investigating Titan's subsurface sea and the unexpected difficulties confronted. She highlights the verifiable meaning of mankind's investigation underneath the outer layer of an extraterrestrial sea and the significance of flexibility even with vulnerability. The investigation turns into a demonstration of human creativity and versatility, pushing the limits of how we might interpret the universe.

The experience with surprising land developments and varieties in the structure of the sea floor adds layers of intricacy to the logical talk inside the group. Dr. Emily Chang, Dr. Alan Rodriguez, and Dr. Marcus Thompson team up to translate the ramifications of these revelations, perceiving that Titan's subsurface sea is a dynamic and developing climate. The chasm, when seen as a static domain, turns into a demonstration of the powerful exchange of topographical and possibly natural cycles inside an extraterrestrial sea.

The Titan Explorer's automated arms, controlled with accuracy by Dr. Alan Rodriguez and his group, become instruments of logical request, gathering tests and directing investigations that add to the developing collection of information about Titan's subsurface geography. The specific cameras, intended for organic investigation under the management of Dr. Marcus Thompson, catch pictures of Titan's submerged domain, giving a visual story of the extraterrestrial sea. The pit, when a riddle, turns into an embroidery of land miracles and likely natural secrets.

As the Titan Explorer investigates the sea floor, the group experiences surprising land includes that allude to the moon's dynamic past. Dr. Emily Chang, drawing on her land mastery, teams up with Dr. Alan Rodriguez and the imaging group to dissect the information and pictures communicated by the submarine. The unforeseen land arrangements brief the group to reconsider how they might interpret Titan's subsurface climate, stressing the powerful idea of extraterrestrial investigation.

The Titan Explorer's automated arms, controlled with accuracy by Dr. Alan Rodriguez and his group, become instruments of logical request, gathering tests and directing investigations that add to the developing collection of information about Titan's subsurface geography. The specific cameras, intended for organic investigation under the management of Dr. Marcus Thompson, catch pictures of Titan's submerged domain, giving a visual story of the extraterrestrial sea. The chasm, when a riddle, turns into an embroidery of land miracles and expected organic secrets.

As the Titan Explorer investigates the pit, the group uncovers surprising varieties in the structure and temperature of the fluid hydrocarbons.

Dr. Emily Chang, teaming up with Dr. Alan Rodriguez, examines the information sent by the sub, endeavoring to unwind the secrets of Titan's subsurface climate. The specialized difficulties of deciphering the information progressively become a powerful course of logical request, provoking the group to change their speculations and investigate the unexplored world.

The versatility of the Titan Explorer group is obvious as the submarine explores through the chasm, defeating specialized obstacles and unanticipated difficulties. Dr. Victoria Hayes, tending to the group at mission control, recognizes the intricacies of the plummet and the surprising disclosures made. She highlights the significance of versatility and cooperation, underscoring that the mission's prosperity lies in affirming existing speculations as well as in embracing the extraordinary capability of startling discoveries.

The experience with unforeseen land arrangements and varieties in the piece of the fluid hydrocarbons adds layers of intricacy to the logical talk inside the group. Dr. Emily Chang, Dr. Alan Rodriguez, and Dr. Hayden Carter team up to translate the ramifications of these revelations, perceiving that Titan's subsurface climate is a dynamic and developing framework. The chasm, when seen as a static domain, turns into a demonstration of the powerful transaction of land processes inside an extraterrestrial sea.

The Titan Explorer's plummet into the void turns into an excursion of divulging Titan's privileged insights, with every revelation testing assumptions and extending the skylines of human information. The geographical marvels and surprising varieties in the sythesis of Titan's subsurface sea become basic parts of the advancing story. Dr. Victoria Hayes, driving the group with key vision, empowers the soul of investigation and interest that characterizes humankind's mission for figuring out the secrets of the universe.

The Titan Explorer's drop into the void turns into a vital part in Sub Stories Titan's Maritime Investigation. The group's capacity to adjust to the powerful climate of Titan's subsurface, conquer specialized difficulties, and make momentous disclosures highlights the flexibility and assurance that drive logical investigation. Dr. Victoria Hayes, thinking about the excursion, welcomes humankind to partake in the fervor of divulging Titan's mysteries and to embrace the continuous experience of investigating the astronomical unexplored world.

6.3 Scientific breakthroughs and surprises that challenge previous assumptions.

The investigation of Titan's subsurface sea by the Titan Explorer prompts a progression of logical leap forwards and shocks that challenge past suspicions, reshaping's comprehension humankind might interpret this cryptic moon of Saturn. Dr. Victoria Hayes, at the very front of the mission, directs a group of researchers, specialists, and voyagers through an excursion of remarkable disclosure.

Commandant James Mitchell, directing the Titan Explorer with accuracy, works together with Dr. Hayden Carter, administering the drive framework, to explore through the intricacies of Titan's subsurface climate. The impetus framework, finely tuned for versatility, answers Administrator Mitchell's orders as the sub adventures further into the moon's secret sea. The group at mission control, including Dr. Sophia

Ramirez overseeing correspondence, enthusiastically anticipates every disclosure with a blend of energy and logical expectation.

As the Titan Explorer dives into the profundities of Titan's subsurface sea, the principal shock comes as unforeseen geographical highlights. Dr. Emily Chang, the geologist, teams up with Commandant Mitchell to decipher the developing scene caught by the sensors. High-goal pictures uncover mind boggling arrangements, testing earlier presumptions about the moon's geographical history. Dr. Chang's topographical mastery becomes instrumental in disentangling the mysteries of Titan's subsurface, transforming each shock into a critical piece of the land puzzle.

Dr. Alan Rodriguez assumes command over the automated arms, intended for accuracy and versatility in Titan's difficult climate. The group faces the specialized test of associating with the submerged scene, gathering tests, and leading topographical investigations. Dr. Rodriguez organizes the sending of the mechanical arms, changing the pit into a logical lab for the careful assessment of Titan's subsurface creation.

Unforeseen natural discoveries add an additional layer of shock to the investigation. Dr. Marcus Thompson, regulating the natural investigation, coordinates the specific cameras towards potential areas of interest that might hold onto indications of something going on under the surface. The hydrocarbon-rich climate, once thought to be cold, turns into a material for expected organic disclosures. Dr. Thompson examines the pictures for any indications of development or designs that might show the presence of life in Titan's subsurface sea. The specialized difficulties of imaging in Titan's barometrical circumstances add intricacy to the organic investigation.

The Titan Explorer's process through Titan's subsurface sea turns into a visual display as the particular cameras catch the ethereal magnificence of the extraterrestrial domain. Dr. Marcus Thompson, investigating the natural information, works together with Dr. Alan Rodriguez and Dr. Emily Chang to correspond the natural discoveries with the land highlights. The transaction among science and geography turns into a point of convergence of request, inciting the group to investigate the possible associations between Titan's subsurface cycles and the presence of life.

Varieties in the structure and temperature of the sea depths present startling difficulties. Dr. Hayden Carter, supervising the drive framework, teams up with Authority James Mitchell to explore through areas of expected disturbance and strange land highlights.

The specialized difficulties of changing the submarine's way while keeping up with strength become a unique part of the investigation, exhibiting the versatility of the designing arrangements executed in the Titan Explorer.

Dr. Victoria Hayes, tending to the group at mission control, recognizes the intricacies of investigating Titan's subsurface sea and the unexpected difficulties confronted. She highlights the verifiable meaning of mankind's investigation underneath the outer layer of an extraterrestrial sea and the significance of flexibility notwithstanding vulnerability. The investigation turns into a demonstration of human inventiveness and strength, pushing the limits of how we might interpret the universe.

Unforeseen amazements keep on arising as the Titan Explorer investigates the subsurface sea. Land arrangements and varieties in the creation of the sea depths challenge assumptions about Titan's topography. Dr. Emily Chang, Dr. Alan Rodriguez, and Dr. Hayden Carter team up to translate the ramifications of these disclosures, perceiving that Titan's subsurface is a dynamic and developing climate. The pit, when seen as a static domain, turns into a demonstration of the powerful transaction of geographical cycles inside an extraterrestrial sea.

The Titan Explorer's mechanical arms, controlled with accuracy by Dr. Alan Rodriguez and his group, become instruments of logical request, gathering tests and leading examinations that add to the developing assemblage of information about Titan's subsurface geography. The particular cameras, intended for organic investigation under the management of Dr. Marcus Thompson, catch pictures of Titan's submerged domain, giving a visual story of the extraterrestrial sea. The chasm, when a mystery, turns into an embroidery of geographical miracles and possible natural secrets.

As the Titan Explorer investigates the pit, the group reveals amazing varieties in the sythesis and temperature of the fluid hydrocarbons. Dr. Emily Chang, working together with Dr. Alan Rodriguez, breaks down the information communicated by the submarine, endeavoring to unwind the secrets of Titan's subsurface climate. The specialized difficulties of deciphering the information continuously become a unique course of logical request, provoking the group to change their speculations and investigate the unexplored world.

The versatility of the Titan Explorer group is clear as the sub explores through the pit, beating specialized obstacles and unexpected difficulties. Dr. Victoria Hayes, tending to the group at mission control, recognizes the intricacies of the plummet and the startling disclosures made. She highlights the significance of flexibility and joint effort, stressing that the mission's prosperity lies in affirming existing speculations as well as in embracing the groundbreaking capability of unforeseen discoveries.

The experience with unforeseen geographical developments, organic revelations, and varieties in the organization of the sea floor adds layers of intricacy to the logical talk inside the group. Dr. Emily Chang, Dr. Alan Rodriguez, and Dr. Marcus Thompson team up to translate the ramifications of these disclosures, perceiving that Titan's subsurface is a dynamic and developing framework. The pit, when seen as a static domain, turns into a demonstration of the powerful transaction of geographical and possibly natural cycles inside an extraterrestrial sea.

The Titan Explorer's plunge into the chasm turns into an excursion of logical forward leaps and shocks, testing past suppositions and growing the skylines of human information. The topographical miracles, unforeseen organic discoveries, and varieties in the sythesis of Titan's subsurface sea become vital parts of the advancing story. Dr. Victoria Hayes, driving the group with key vision, supports the soul of investigation and interest that characterizes humankind's journey for grasping the secrets of the universe.

The Titan Explorer's plunge into the chasm turns into a vital part in Submarine Stories Titan's Maritime Investigation. The group's capacity to adjust to the powerful climate of Titan's subsurface, defeat specialized difficulties, and make momentous disclosures highlights the versatility and assurance that drive logical investigation. Dr. Victoria Hayes, thinking about the excursion, welcomes mankind to partake in the fervor of the logical leap forwards and shocks that reclassify how we might interpret Titan's subsurface sea and to embrace the continuous experience of investigating the enormous unexplored world.

Chapter 7

Deep-Sea Drama

The Titan Explorer, exploring the strange profundities of Titan's subsurface sea, experiences a progression of remote ocean shows that spellbind the group furthermore, rethink the mission's account. Dr. Victoria Hayes, the visionary chief initiating this extraordinary campaign, guides the group through the unpredictable difficulties presented by the moon of Saturn.

Commandant James Mitchell, entrusted with the sensitive route of the Titan Explorer, teams up intimately with Dr. Hayden Carter, administering the impetus framework. As the sub dives further into Titan's secret sea, the impetus framework answers with accuracy to Administrator Mitchell's orders, showing the consistent cooperative energy between human aptitude and state of the art innovation. The group at mission control, including Dr. Sophia Ramirez overseeing correspondence, anticipates every improvement with a blend of expectation and logical interest.

The main demonstration of this remote ocean show unfurls as unforeseen land highlights come into center. Dr. Emily Chang, the geologist, teams up with Commandant Mitchell to decipher the advancing scene caught by the sensors.

High-goal pictures uncover a unique submerged landscape, set apart by transcending mountains and huge fields, testing assumptions about Titan's topographical history. Dr. Chang's land discernment becomes instrumental in deciphering the topographical show unfurling underneath the frosty outside layer, transforming every disclosure into a section in Titan's old story.

Dr. Alan Rodriguez, the genius behind the automated arms, becomes the overwhelming focus in the following demonstration. These accuracy instruments, intended for flexibility in Titan's difficult climate, become vital participants in the show. The group faces the specialized test of cooperating with the submerged scene, gathering tests, and directing geographical investigations. Dr. Rodriguez coordinates the organization of the mechanical arms, changing the pit into a logical theater where the insider facts of Titan's subsurface structure are uncovered with each painstakingly executed development.

Surprising natural disclosures add a component of tension to the unfurling remote ocean show. Dr. Marcus Thompson, managing the natural investigation, coordinates the particular cameras towards potential areas of interest that might hold onto indications of something going on under the surface. The once-thought unwelcoming, hydrocarbon-rich climate turns into a phase for possible natural disclosures. Dr. Thompson examines the pictures for any indications of development or designs that might show the presence of life in Titan's subsurface sea. The specialized difficulties of imaging in Titan's environmental circumstances add intricacy to the natural investigation, uplifting the expectation of what the specific cameras could catch.

The Titan Explorer's process through Titan's subsurface sea turns into a visual exhibition as the particular cameras catch the ethereal magnificence of the extraterrestrial domain. Dr. Marcus Thompson, investigating the natural information, works together with Dr. Alan Rodriguez and Dr. Emily Chang to correspond the natural discoveries with the land highlights. The exchange among science and geography turns into a point of convergence of request, adding layers to the unfurling show and provoking the group to investigate the possible associations between Titan's subsurface cycles and the presence of life.

The show escalates as varieties in the piece and temperature of the sea depths come to the front. Dr. Hayden Carter, regulating the impetus framework, teams up with Leader James Mitchell to explore through areas of expected choppiness and unfamiliar land highlights. The specialized difficulties of changing the submarine's way while keeping up with security become a powerful part of the investigation, displaying the flexibility of the designing arrangements executed in the Titan Explorer. The crowd at mission control is as eager and anxious as ever as the sub moves through the exciting bends in the road of Titan's submerged scene.

Dr. Victoria Hayes, tending to the group at mission control, recognizes the intricacies of investigating Titan's subsurface sea and the unanticipated difficulties confronted. She highlights the verifiable meaning of humankind's investigation underneath the outer layer of an extraterrestrial sea and the significance of flexibility despite vulnerability. The investigation turns into a demonstration of human creativity and flexibility, pushing the limits of how we might interpret the universe.

Unforeseen land arrangements, organic disclosures, and varieties in the structure of the sea depths add layers of intricacy to the logical talk inside the group. Dr. Emily Chang, Dr. Alan Rodriguez, and Dr. Marcus Thompson team up to translate the ramifications of these disclosures, perceiving that Titan's subsurface is a dynamic and developing climate. The void, when seen as a static domain, turns into a demonstration of the unique exchange of geographical and possibly natural cycles inside an extraterrestrial sea.

The Titan Explorer's plummet into the chasm turns into an excursion of remote ocean show, with every disclosure testing past suspicions and reshaping the story of Titan's subsurface investigation. The topographical marvels, unforeseen organic discoveries, and varieties in the arrangement of Titan's subsurface sea become necessary parts of the advancing story. Dr. Victoria Hayes, driving the group with vital vision, empowers the soul of investigation and interest that characterizes mankind's journey for figuring out the secrets of the universe.

The show takes a thrilling turn as the Titan Explorer experiences unforeseen varieties in the sythesis and temperature of the fluid hydrocarbons. Dr. Emily Chang, teaming up with Dr. Alan Rodriguez, examines the information sent by the submarine, endeavoring to unwind the secrets of Titan's subsurface climate. The specialized difficulties of deciphering the information continuously become a unique course of logical request, inciting the group to change their speculations and investigate the unexplored world.

The versatility of the Titan Explorer group is clear as the submarine explores through the void, beating specialized obstacles and unexpected difficulties. Dr. Victoria Hayes, tending to the group at mission control, recognizes the intricacies of the drop and the startling disclosures made. She highlights the significance of versatility and joint effort, underlining that the mission's prosperity lies in affirming existing speculations as well as in embracing the groundbreaking capability of unforeseen discoveries.

The remote ocean show keeps on unfurling as the Titan Explorer investigates the subsurface sea. Geographical developments, organic secrets, and varieties in the sythesis of the sea depths present an enthralling story that rises above the limits of human information.

Dr. Emily Chang, Dr. Alan Rodriguez, and Dr. Marcus Thompson team up to unravel the ramifications of these revelations, perceiving that Titan's subsurface is a dynamic and developing framework. The pit, when seen as a static domain, turns into a phase for the continuous investigation of Titan's mysteries.

The Titan Explorer's drop into the chasm turns into an excursion of remote ocean show, with every disclosure testing assumptions and growing the skylines of human information. The land ponders, surprising natural discoveries, and varieties in the sythesis of Titan's subsurface sea become necessary parts of the advancing story. Dr. Victoria Hayes, driving the group with key vision, supports the soul of investigation and interest that characterizes mankind's mission for grasping the secrets of the universe.

As the remote ocean show unfurls, the group wrestles with the unforeseen, embracing the difficulties and shocks experienced in Titan's subsurface sea. Dr. Victoria Hayes, thinking about the excursion, recognizes the extraordinary force of remote ocean investigation and the strength of the human soul even with the unexplored world. The Titan Explorer group turns into an aggregate hero in this enormous show, exploring unfamiliar waters and revising the content of extraterrestrial investigation.

In the last venture of the remote ocean show, the Titan Explorer rises out of the void, carrying with it a store of logical disclosures that rethink's comprehension humankind might interpret Titan's subsurface sea. Dr. Victoria Hayes, tending to the world from mission control, shares the group's victories and difficulties, welcoming humankind to participate in the energy of unwinding the secrets of an outsider world.

The remote ocean show of Titan's maritime investigation turns into a demonstration of human interest, determination, and the ceaseless journey to investigate the infinite unexplored world.

7.1 Unexpected challenges and dangers arise as Titan Voyager explores deeper.

As the Titan Explorer sets out on its main goal to investigate the profundities of Titan's subsurface sea, the unfurling story goes off in a strange direction, giving the group unexpected difficulties and risks that add a layer of intricacy to the vast undertaking. Dr. Victoria Hayes, the visionary chief initiating the mission, directs the different group of researchers, specialists, and travelers through unfamiliar waters on Saturn's biggest moon.

Authority James Mitchell, liable for the sensitive route of the Titan Explorer, teams up intimately with Dr. Hayden Carter, directing the impetus framework. The submarine, intended for flexibility in Titan's difficult climate, answers with accuracy to Leader Mitchell's orders as it adventures further into the moon's secret sea.

The group at mission control, including Dr. Sophia Ramirez overseeing correspondence, anticipates every improvement with a blend of energy and logical expectation.

Startling topographical highlights mark the underlying phases of the investigation, dazzling Dr. Emily Chang, the geologist, who teams up with Officer Mitchell to decipher the developing scene caught by the sensors. High-goal pictures uncover a powerful submerged territory, described by transcending mountains and immense fields, testing assumptions about Titan's geographical history. Dr. Chang's topographical mastery becomes instrumental in unraveling the secrets of Titan's subsurface, transforming every disclosure into a part in the moon's land story.

The story accepts an unanticipated wind as the Titan Explorer experiences unforeseen varieties in the structure and temperature of the sea floor. Dr. Hayden Carter, regulating the impetus framework, teams up with Administrator James Mitchell to explore through locales of expected disturbance and unfamiliar land highlights. The specialized difficulties of changing the submarine's way while keeping up with soundness become a unique part of the investigation, exhibiting the versatility of the designing arrangements executed in the Titan Explorer.

As the Titan Explorer investigates further, the group faces a flood of unforeseen difficulties. Geographical arrangements, recently remembered to be static, uncover dynamic and erratic qualities. Dr. Emily Chang, Dr. Alan Rodriguez, and Dr. Marcus Thompson team up to interpret the ramifications of these revelations, perceiving that Titan's subsurface is a complex and developing framework. The void, when seen as a generally steady climate, turns into a proving ground for the group's flexibility and critical thinking abilities.

Dr. Alan Rodriguez, the driving force behind the mechanical arms, becomes the overwhelming focus in tending to the raising difficulties. These accuracy instruments, intended for flexibility in Titan's flighty climate, become urgent apparatuses in exploring through the startling topographical elements. The group faces the overwhelming assignment of gathering tests, directing examinations, and adjusting the submarine's way because of the unique idea of Titan's subsurface sea. Dr. Rodriguez organizes the organization of the mechanical arms, changing the chasm into a logical theater where the group should make do and enhance continuously.

In the midst of the land shocks, Dr. Marcus Thompson, regulating the natural investigation, coordinates the particular cameras towards potential areas of interest that might hold onto indications of something going on under the surface. The hydrocarbon-rich climate, once thought to be cold, turns into a domain of elevated organic interest. Dr. Thompson examines the pictures for any indications of development or designs that might demonstrate the presence of life in Titan's subsurface sea. The specialized difficulties of imaging in Titan's climatic circumstances add an additional layer of intricacy to the natural investigation, as the group wrestles with the unforeseen turns in the story.

The Titan Explorer's process through Titan's subsurface sea turns into a strained and capricious show as the particular cameras catch the developing magnificence of the extraterrestrial domain. Dr. Marcus Thompson, investigating the organic information, teams up with Dr. Alan Rodriguez and Dr. Emily Chang to correspond the organic discoveries with the geographical elements. The transaction among science and geography turns into a point of convergence of request, as the group explores through the intricacies of Titan's subsurface climate, adjusting to the startling difficulties that emerge.

The story takes an emotional turn as the Titan Explorer faces unanticipated risks as tempestuous locales and outrageous varieties in pressure. Dr. Victoria Hayes, tending to the group at mission control, recognizes the increased dangers of investigating further into Titan's subsurface sea. She highlights the significance of versatility, coordinated effort, and wariness as the group stands up to the unexplored world. The investigation turns into a trial of human versatility and resourcefulness, with each colleague adding to the unfurling show with their mastery and critical thinking abilities.

Unforeseen varieties in the piece and temperature of the fluid hydrocarbons represent another arrangement of difficulties for the group. Dr. Emily Chang, working together with Dr. Alan Rodriguez, dissects the information sent by the sub, endeavoring to unwind the secrets of Titan's subsurface climate. The specialized difficulties of deciphering the information progressively become a powerful course of logical request, provoking the group to change their speculations and explore through the unknown waters of Titan's sea.

The strength of the Titan Explorer group is apparent as the submarine explores through the chasm, conquering specialized obstacles and unexpected risks. Dr. Victoria Hayes, tending to the group at mission control, recognizes the intricacies of the plunge and the unforeseen difficulties confronted. She highlights the significance of flexibility and cooperation, accentuating that the mission's prosperity lies in affirming existing speculations as well as in embracing the extraordinary capability of surprising discoveries.

As the Titan Explorer investigates further, the group experiences unfamiliar districts and outrageous circumstances that test the restrictions of the sub and its team. The startling provokes become vital to the unfurling dramatization, exhibiting the group's capacity to adjust and issue settle continuously. Dr. Victoria Hayes, driving the group with key vision, supports the soul of investigation and interest that characterizes humankind's mission for figuring out the secrets of the universe.

The Titan Explorer's plunge into the chasm turns into an arresting section in Submarine Stories Titan's Maritime Investigation. The group's capacity to explore through the unforeseen difficulties and perils highlights the flexibility and assurance that drive logical investigation.

Dr. Victoria Hayes, considering the excursion, welcomes mankind to partake in the fervor of investigating the enormous obscure and to embrace the continuous experience of unwinding the secrets concealed underneath Titan's cold outside.

In the peak of the surprising show, the Titan Explorer rises up out of the profundities of Titan's subsurface sea, carrying with it a stash of logical disclosures and a demonstration of human resourcefulness and persistence. Dr. Victoria Hayes, tending to the world from mission control, shares the group's victories and difficulties, underlining the unusual idea of remote ocean investigation on an extraterrestrial moon. The startling difficulties and perils become piece of the account, molding the aggregate story of mankind's investigation of the astronomical outskirts.

7.2 Technical malfunctions, encounters with hostile creatures, and the resilience of the team in overcoming crises.

The Titan Explorer's excursion into the profundities of Titan's subsurface sea takes a sensational turn as the group experiences a progression of surprising difficulties, including specialized glitches, experiences with unfriendly animals, and the striking flexibility of the group in defeating emergencies. Dr. Victoria Hayes, the spearheading pioneer in charge of the mission, directs the different group through unfamiliar domains on Saturn's biggest moon.

Authority James Mitchell, liable for the exact route of the Titan Explorer, teams up intimately with Dr. Hayden Carter, managing the impetus framework. As the sub plunges into the moon's secret sea, specialized glitches emerge, testing the group's aptitude and flexibility. The impetus framework, finely tuned for versatility in Titan's difficult climate, experiences unforeseen errors. Authority Mitchell and Dr. Carter work energetically to investigate and recalibrate the framework, featuring the fragile dance between human control and cutting edge innovation in the unforgiving profundities.

Despite specialized breakdowns, the group at mission control, including Dr. Sophia Ramirez overseeing correspondence, assumes a vital part in offering help and mastery. The difficulties presented by the breaking down impetus framework become an ongoing trial of the group's critical thinking abilities and versatility. Dr. Victoria Hayes, tending to the group, accentuates the significance of collaboration and fast reasoning in beating specialized obstacles. The investigation turns into a demonstration of human inventiveness as the group teams up to reestablish the usefulness of the Titan Explorer and keep the mission on course.

As the Titan Explorer proceeds with its drop, experiences with threatening animals add a layer of tension to the unfurling story. Dr. Marcus Thompson, supervising the organic investigation, coordinates the particular cameras towards potential areas of interest that might hold onto indications of something going on under the surface.

Startlingly, the cameras catch looks at antagonistic animals, adjusted to the unforgiving states of Titan's subsurface sea. Dr. Thompson and the group face the test of exploring through districts occupied by these strange creatures, adding a component of risk to the grandiose investigation.

The Titan Explorer's process through Titan's subsurface sea turns into a high-stakes experience as the specific cameras catch the unfriendly animals right at home. Dr. Marcus Thompson, dissecting the natural information, works together with Dr. Alan Rodriguez and Dr. Emily Chang to devise procedures for securely exploring through locales populated by these obscure living things. The interchange among science and innovation turns into a pivotal part of the mission, featuring the intricacies of investigating extraterrestrial conditions with likely occupants.

Specialized breakdowns and experiences with unfriendly animals stretch the group to the edges of their versatility. Dr. Victoria Hayes, tending to the group at mission control, recognizes the difficulties confronted and compliments the aggregate assurance to beat emergencies. She highlights the unconventionality of remote ocean investigation on an extraterrestrial moon and the mental fortitude expected to explore through unknown domains. The investigation turns into a demonstration of human flexibility and the unwavering soul of investigation.

As the group faces specialized breakdowns and explores through locales occupied by threatening animals, Dr. Alan Rodriguez, managing the mechanical arms, assumes a vital part in guaranteeing the security and progress of the mission. The mechanical arms, intended for accuracy and flexibility, become fundamental apparatuses in exploring through testing conditions and gathering tests for examination. Dr. Rodriguez and his cooperation carefully to send the mechanical arms, exhibiting the significance of mechanical mastery in beating the surprising difficulties presented by the vast investigation.

The flexibility of the Titan Explorer group is obvious as they explore through the profundities of Titan's subsurface sea, defeating specialized breakdowns and adjusting to the presence of unfriendly animals. Dr. Victoria Hayes, tending to the world from mission control, shares the group's victories and difficulties, underlining the capricious idea of remote ocean investigation on an extraterrestrial moon. The specialized breakdowns and experiences with threatening animals become vital parts of the account, forming the aggregate story of humankind's investigation of the grandiose outskirts.

In the last venture of this grandiose show, the Titan Explorer rises out of the pit, carrying with it a stash of logical disclosures and a demonstration of the group's versatility despite unexpected difficulties. Dr. Victoria Hayes, tending to the group and the worldwide crowd, praises the victories of the mission and recognizes the significant illustrations gained from conquering emergencies. The specialized glitches and experiences with unfriendly animals become parts in the continuous story of human investigation, featuring the unstoppable soul that drives mankind into the grandiose unexplored world.

7.3 The emotional toll on the crew as they face the unknown.

As the Titan Explorer dives further into the unfamiliar waters of Titan's subsurface sea, the profound cost for the group becomes substantial, winding around a nuanced story of expectation, uneasiness, and strength. Dr. Victoria Hayes, the sturdy chief directing the mission, perceives the significant effect of confronting the obscure in the different group of researchers, architects, and voyagers.

Commandant James Mitchell, entrusted with the sensitive route of the Titan Explorer, feels the heaviness of obligation as the sub experiences unanticipated difficulties. The profound cost appears in snapshots of calm examination and extreme concentration as Commandant Mitchell explores through the outsider landscape underneath Titan's frigid covering. The seclusion of the remote ocean climate uplifts the close to home power, making a feeling of weakness for both the group and the sub.

Specialized breakdowns, experienced during the drop, add an additional layer of profound intricacy. Dr. Hayden Carter, directing the impetus framework, encounters a blend of disappointment and assurance as the group wrestles with startling errors. The profound cost of investigating and recalibrating the impetus framework is apparent in the wrinkled temples and traded looks among the group at mission control. Dr. Sophia Ramirez, overseeing correspondence, assumes an imperative part in keeping up with the close to home harmony by cultivating clear correspondence channels in the midst of the specialized difficulties.

As the Titan Explorer proceeds with its drop, experiences with threatening animals enhance the profound stakes. Dr. Marcus Thompson, regulating the natural investigation, recognizes the increased feeling of stunningness and fear among the group. The profound cost of experiencing obscure life structures neglected, dim profundities of Titan's sea resonates through the sub. Dr. Thompson, deciphering the organic information, turns into a conductor for the profound responses of the team, making an interpretation of the logical disclosures into a common human encounter.

Dr. Emily Chang, the geologist, ends up sincerely snared with the outsider scenes uncovered by high-goal pictures. The startling topographical highlights challenge her predispositions and light a feeling of marvel that rises above the limits of logical request. The profound cost for Dr. Chang turns into a demonstration of the profoundly special interaction fashioned with Titan's old topographical history.

Amidst specialized glitches and experiences with threatening animals, the profound flexibility of the group arises as a principal quality. Dr. Alan Rodriguez, managing the mechanical arms, turns into a mainstay of solidarity as he coordinates accuracy moves to explore through testing conditions.

The profound cost for Dr. Rodriguez is clear in the wrinkled temples and centered assurance as he sends the automated arms with careful accuracy, encapsulating the group's aggregate purpose despite misfortune.

Dr. Victoria Hayes, tending to the group at mission control, recognizes the close to home cost of the mission and highlights the significance of supporting each other. The remote ocean show unfurling underneath Titan's frosty outside layer turns into a common excursion, cultivating a feeling of fellowship among the team. Dr. Hayes, with compassion and understanding, perceives that confronting the obscure isn't simply a logical undertaking however a profoundly close to home experience that ties the group together.

As the Titan Explorer investigates further into the subsurface sea, the close to home cost stretches out past the specialized difficulties and experiences with obscure living things. The disengagement, the tension of disentangling extraterrestrial secrets, and the vulnerability of what lies ahead make an extraordinary profound scene for each group part. Dr. Marcus Thompson, digging into the natural information, considers the profound range from amazement to anxiety, recognizing the human component woven into the logical texture of the mission.

The flexibility of the Titan Explorer group radiates through as they explore the close to home intricacies of the vast investigation. Dr. Victoria Hayes, with a sharp comprehension of the human mind, cultivates a climate of open correspondence and everyday encouragement. The group's common encounters, from snapshots of wonderment to the difficulties of investigating, become the profound strings that weave a story of brotherhood, trust, and shared regard.

In the last venture of the close to home show, the Titan Explorer rises up out of the pit, carrying with it a store of logical disclosures and an aggregate feeling of win. Dr. Victoria Hayes, tending to the world from mission control, recognizes the profound cost for the team and welcomes mankind to partake in the sensational excursion. The close to home intricacy of confronting the obscure turns into a focal subject in the story of Titan's maritime investigation, featuring the unyielding soul of human investigation.

Chapter 8

The Abyssal Gateway

As the Titan Explorer proceeds with its entrancing plummet into the neglected profundities of Titan's subsurface sea, the story takes a dazzling turn, presenting the idea of the "Deep Passage" - a term begat by Dr. Victoria Hayes to embody a puzzling locale that holds the potential for earth shattering revelations and extraordinary difficulties. Dr. Hayes, the visionary chief initiating the mission, perceives the meaning of this deep domain as the group explores through the frosty outside layer of Saturn's biggest moon.

Leader James Mitchell, liable for the exact route of the Titan Explorer, detects the elevated expectation and strain among the team as they approach the Deep Entryway. The actual term brings out a feeling of wonderment and fear, catching the pith of wandering into an obscure and possibly unpredictable area. The profound cost for Leader Mitchell and the group becomes unmistakable as they stand on the limit of an infinite door that guarantees both logical disclosures and unanticipated difficulties.

Dr. Hayden Carter, directing the drive framework, assumes a basic part in setting up the Titan Explorer for the excursion through the Deep Door. The impetus framework, finely tuned for versatility in Titan's difficult climate, faces the one of a kind requests of this unknown locale.

Specialized complexities add an additional layer of intricacy to the investigation, and Dr. Carter teams up with Officer Mitchell to guarantee the submarine is prepared to explore through the pit with accuracy.

As the Titan Explorer moves toward the Deep Entryway, Dr. Emily Chang, the geologist, anxiously anticipates the topographical miracles that might unfurl in this neglected area. High-goal pictures uncover a supernatural scene set apart by transcending arrangements and land includes that overcome traditional presumption. Dr. Chang's land skill becomes instrumental in translating the mysterious geographical cycles forming the Deep Passage, adding a layer of logical interest to the grandiose excursion.

The idea of the Deep Entryway reaches out past the land domain, enveloping possible organic revelations in the hydrocarbon-rich climate. Dr. Marcus Thompson, regulating the organic investigation, coordinates the specific cameras towards locales that might hold onto indications of something going on under the surface. The expectation among the group arrives at a crescendo as the cameras catch looks at special living things adjusted to the outrageous states of the Deep Passage. Dr. Thompson's mastery in science turns into a directing light as the group explores through the sensitive equilibrium between logical request and moral contemplations.

Dr. Alan Rodriguez, the brains behind the automated arms, becomes the dominant focal point in setting up the Titan Explorer for associations inside the Deep Entryway. The versatility of the automated arms becomes critical as the group faces the test of gathering tests and directing examinations in this neglected domain. Dr. Rodriguez coordinates the organization of the mechanical arms, changing the void into a logical theater where the group should explore through the obscure with accuracy and artfulness.

The close to home intricacy of moving toward the Deep Door is highlighted by Dr. Sophia Ramirez, overseeing correspondence at mission control. The correspondence interface turns into a life saver as the Titan Explorer wanders into the profundities where signs might confront impedance or postponements. The profound cost for Dr. Ramirez becomes obvious as she keeps up with clear correspondence channels, giving a constant flow of data and backing to the team exploring through the Deep Entryway.

As the Titan Explorer passes the boundary of the Deep Entryway, the story takes on a strange quality. The neglected district uncovers itself with an ensemble of geographical developments, special living things, and varieties in the piece of Titan's subsurface sea. Dr. Victoria Hayes, tending to the group and the worldwide crowd from mission control, recognizes the authentic meaning of this vast door. The Deep Door turns into a representation for humankind's ceaseless mission to push the limits of investigation and understanding.

Specialized difficulties inside the Deep Door test the restrictions of the Titan Explorer and the strength of the group. Officer James Mitchell, exploring a through the strange area, faces unforeseen varieties in pressure and unfamiliar land highlights. The profound cost for Administrator Mitchell is reflected in the aggregate purpose of the group at mission control, who witness the sub exploring through the difficulties of the Deep Passage with steadfast assurance.

Dr. Victoria Hayes, perceiving the close to home and logical meaning of the Deep Entryway, encourages a feeling of solidarity and reason among the group. The enormous excursion turns into a common undertaking as the group investigates the secrets concealed inside the frigid profundities of Titan's subsurface sea. Dr. Hayes, with a significant comprehension of the human soul, urges the group to embrace the vulnerabilities of the Deep Entryway and change difficulties into open doors for logical forward leaps.

The natural investigation inside the Deep Passage adds a layer of profound intricacy as the specific cameras catch new life frames that overcome regular presumption. Dr. Marcus Thompson, breaking down the natural information, teams up with Dr. Emily Chang and Dr. Alan Rodriguez to decipher the ramifications of these revelations. The close to home cost for the group is clear as they wrestle with the significant ramifications of experiencing life in an extraterrestrial sea, reshaping the story of Titan's subsurface investigation.

The land ponders inside the Deep Door become a visual exhibition as high-goal pictures uncover complex developments and topographical cycles. Dr. Emily Chang, drenched in the land information, teams up with Administrator James Mitchell to unravel the geographical history carved into the cold outside layer of Titan. The close to home cost for Dr. Chang is a combination of logical miracle and the acknowledgment that the Deep Passage holds the way to disentangling the enormous secrets concealed inside Saturn's biggest moon.

Dr. Alan Rodriguez, supervising the mechanical arms, turns into an image of versatility and accuracy as the group conducts complex moves inside the Deep Passage. The profound intricacy of communicating with the obscure is reflected in the engaged assurance of Dr. Rodriguez and his group. The mechanical arms, expansions of human inventiveness, explore through the outsider scene, gathering tests and leading investigations that add to the advancing account of Titan's subsurface investigation.

As the Titan Explorer explores through the Deep Door, the close to home cost for the team turns into a focal subject in the unfurling story. Dr. Victoria Hayes, considering the aggregate excursion, recognizes the profound ups and downs that characterize the investigation of the inestimable unexplored world. The Deep Entryway, with its land marvels and likely natural disclosures, turns into a cauldron of human feelings, testing the strength and soul of the group.

In the last venture of this enormous show, the Titan Explorer rises out of the Deep Passage, carrying with it a stash of logical revelations and a significant comprehension of the close to home intricacies innate in investigating the vast unexplored world. Dr. Victoria Hayes, tending to the world from mission control, welcomes mankind to partake in the victories and difficulties of exploring the Deep Entryway. The idea turns into an image of humankind's tenacious quest for information and the boldness to face the vulnerabilities that lie past the limits of known investigation.

8.1 The team discovers a mysterious underwater gateway leading to uncharted depths.

In the unfurling adventure of Submarine Stories Titan's Maritime Investigation, the story accepts a thrilling turn as the group on board the Titan Explorer coincidentally finds a strange submerged passage, an until now obscure section guide driving toward unfamiliar profundities of Titan's subsurface sea. Dr. Victoria Hayes, the visionary chief organizing the mission, perceives the great meaning of this revelation as the group leaves on an excursion into the grandiose unexplored world.

Leader James Mitchell, liable for the exact route of the Titan Explorer, encounters a flood of expectation and energy as the submarine methodologies the strange door. The actual term, "The Deep Door," instituted by Dr. Hayes, catches the perplexing idea of this infinite passage point, bringing out a feeling of stunningness and miracle among the team. The profound reverberation is unmistakable as Commandant Mitchell controls the submarine towards this strange entry into Titan's secret profundities.

Dr. Hayden Carter, regulating the impetus framework, turns into a key part in setting up the Titan Explorer for the special difficulties presented by the Deep Entryway. The drive framework, a mechanical wonder finely tuned for versatility in Titan's difficult climate, becomes the dominant focal point as the group considers the complexities of exploring through this puzzling vast entry. Dr. Carter teams up with Administrator Mitchell to guarantee the submarine is prepared to cross the entryway with accuracy and flexibility.

As the Titan Explorer moves toward the Deep Door, Dr. Emily Chang, the geologist, anxiously expects the topographical marvels that might unfurl in this neglected locale. High-goal pictures sent by the sub's high level sensors uncover an uncommon submerged scene set apart by transcending arrangements and land includes already concealed. Dr. Chang's topographical skill turns into a guide of knowledge as the group explores through the stunning geographical embroidery concealed underneath Titan's cold covering.

The idea of the Deep Door stretches out past the geographical domain, consolidating the potential for organic disclosures in this hydrocarbon-rich climate.

Dr. Marcus Thompson, regulating the organic investigation, coordinates specific cameras towards locales that might hold onto indications of something going on under the surface. The group's aggregate energy and anxiety raise as the cameras catch looks at interesting living things adjusted to the outrageous circumstances encompassing the Deep Door. Dr. Thompson turns into an aide, interpreting the potential for organic revelation into an undeniably exhilarating part of the infinite excursion.

Dr. Alan Rodriguez, the genius behind the mechanical arms, expects a crucial job in setting up the Titan Explorer for connections inside the Deep Entryway. The flexibility and accuracy of the automated arms become fundamental devices as the group faces the test of gathering tests and directing examinations in this neglected domain. Dr. Rodriguez coordinates the sending of the mechanical arms, changing the investigation of the passage into an orchestra of innovative artfulness and logical interest.

The close to home intricacy of moving toward the Deep Door is highlighted by Dr. Sophia Ramirez, overseeing correspondence at mission control. The correspondence connect turns into a life saver as the Titan Explorer wanders into the profundities where signs might confront impedance or postponements. Dr. Ramirez's consistent correspondence turns into a wellspring of consolation for the team, featuring the close to home cost and the significance of keeping up with clear correspondence channels in the midst of the vulnerabilities of enormous investigation.

As the Titan Explorer passes the boundary of the Deep Door, the story takes on a dreamlike quality. The neglected district unfurls with an ensemble of geographical developments, novel living things, and varieties in the sythesis of Titan's subsurface sea. Dr. Victoria Hayes, tending to the group and the worldwide crowd from mission control, recognizes the authentic meaning of this enormous door. The Deep Passage turns into a representation for mankind's ceaseless mission to push the limits of investigation and understanding.

Specialized difficulties inside the Deep Door test the constraints of the Titan Explorer and the flexibility of the group. Commandant James Mitchell, exploring a through the strange area, faces surprising varieties in pressure and unfamiliar geographical highlights. The profound cost for Commandant Mitchell is reflected in the aggregate purpose of the group at mission control, who witness the submarine exploring through the difficulties of the Deep Entryway with steady assurance.

Dr. Victoria Hayes, perceiving the profound and logical meaning of the Deep Passage, encourages a feeling of solidarity and reason among the group. The vast excursion turns into a common undertaking as the team investigates the secrets concealed inside the frigid profundities of Titan's subsurface sea. Dr. Hayes, with a significant comprehension of the human soul, urges the group to embrace the vulnerabilities of the Deep Door and change difficulties into open doors for logical leap forwards.

The organic investigation inside the Deep Door adds a layer of profound intricacy as the particular cameras catch new life frames that overcome regular presumption. Dr. Marcus Thompson, breaking down the organic information, works together with Dr. Emily Chang and Dr. Alan Rodriguez to decipher the ramifications of these revelations. The close to home cost for the group is clear as they wrestle with the significant ramifications of experiencing life in an extraterrestrial sea, reshaping the story of Titan's subsurface investigation.

The geographical marvels inside the Deep Door become a visual scene as high-goal pictures uncover multifaceted developments and land processes. Dr. Emily Chang, submerged in the land information, teams up with Administrator James Mitchell to translate the geographical history carved into the frosty outside of Titan. The close to home cost for Dr. Chang is a combination of logical marvel and the acknowledgment that the Deep Door holds the way to unwinding the grandiose secrets concealed inside Saturn's biggest moon.

Dr. Alan Rodriguez, regulating the mechanical arms, turns into an image of versatility and accuracy as the group conducts unpredictable moves inside the Deep Passage. The close to home intricacy of cooperating with the obscure is reflected in the engaged assurance of Dr. Rodriguez and his group. The automated arms, expansions of human resourcefulness, explore through the outsider scene, gathering tests and directing investigations that add to the developing story of Titan's subsurface investigation.

As the Titan Explorer explores through the Deep Entryway, the close to home cost for the group turns into a focal subject in the unfurling story. Dr. Victoria Hayes, thinking about the aggregate excursion, recognizes the close to home ups and downs that characterize the investigation of the astronomical unexplored world. The Deep Entryway, with its land marvels and expected organic disclosures, turns into a cauldron of human feelings, testing the flexibility and soul of the group.

In the last venture of this grandiose show, the Titan Explorer rises up out of the Deep Passage, carrying with it a stash of logical disclosures and a significant comprehension of the profound intricacies intrinsic in investigating the enormous unexplored world. Dr. Victoria Hayes, tending to the world from mission control, welcomes humankind to partake in the victories and difficulties of exploring the Deep Entryway. The idea turns into an image of humankind's constant quest for information and the boldness to stand up to the vulnerabilities that lie past the limits of known investigation.

8.2 Ethical dilemmas and debates about whether to venture into the unknown.

As the Titan Explorer leaves on its remarkable excursion into the profundities of Titan's subsurface sea, a mind boggling trap of moral difficulties and discussions starts to unfurl, testing the actual substance of human investigation. Dr. Victoria Hayes, the directing power behind the mission, ends up at the focal point of these discussions, exploring the fragile harmony between logical interest, moral contemplations, and the obscure secrets that lie ahead.

Leader James Mitchell, entrusted with the exact route of the Titan Explorer, wrestles with the moral components of wandering into strange domains. The obscure dangers present potential dangers not exclusively to the mission yet in addition to the fragile environments that might exist underneath the frigid hull of Titan. The moral issue of whether to continue into these neglected locales turns into a squeezing question, reverberating through the hallways of the space apparatus and mission control.

Dr. Hayden Carter, regulating the drive framework, turns into a vital participant in the moral conversations encompassing the mission. The drive framework, finely tuned for flexibility in Titan's difficult climate, turns into a device that could modify the flawless idea of the subsurface sea. Dr. Carter, torn between the craving for logical investigation and the obligation to safeguard extraterrestrial biological systems, participates in warmed banters inside the group about the expected ecological effect of the Titan Explorer's drive framework.

Dr. Emily Chang, the geologist, faces moral quandaries as the Titan Explorer approaches land ponders inside the obscure profundities. The impulse to extricate tests and lead investigations conflicts with the moral obligation to save the normal province of Titan's subsurface climate. Dr. Chang, with a profound regard for the likely delicacy of extraterrestrial biological systems, turns into a vocal supporter for mindful investigation, setting off banters about the moral limits of logical interest.

The idea of natural investigation inside Titan's subsurface sea presents another layer of moral intricacy. Dr. Marcus Thompson, regulating the organic investigation, defies whether or not the expected disclosure of living things legitimizes the interruption into their natural surroundings. The moral discussions strengthen as the specific cameras catch looks at one of a kind living things adjusted to the outrageous states of Titan's sea, inciting conversations about the expected effect of human investigation on these extraterrestrial biological systems.

Dr. Alan Rodriguez, answerable for the organization and activity of the automated arms, winds up ensnared in moral discussions encompassing the assortment of tests and expected connections with obscure living things.

The sensitive harmony between logical request and moral obligation turns into a focal subject as Dr. Rodriguez explores through the difficulties presented by the outsider scene. The mechanical arms, intended for accuracy, become instruments of moral examination, bringing up issues about the degree to which humankind ought to mediate in the regular request of an extraterrestrial climate.

Dr. Sophia Ramirez, overseeing correspondence at mission control, turns into a middle person in the moral discussions that reverberation between the space apparatus and Earth. The correspondence interface, a life saver between the team and mission control, turns into a channel for the moral contemplations that penetrate each choice. Dr. Ramirez, working with conversations and guaranteeing straightforwardness, assumes an essential part in outlining the moral story of the Titan Explorer mission for a worldwide crowd.

The moral situations looked by the Titan Explorer group reach out past the bounds of the rocket, igniting banters inside established researchers and the more extensive public. Media sources, researchers, ethicists, and tree huggers say something regarding the moral ramifications of wandering into the obscure profundities of Titan's subsurface sea. The inestimable excursion turns into a point of convergence for worldwide conversations about the obligations of mankind as voyagers of the universe.

Dr. Victoria Hayes, perceiving the extent of the moral discussions, requires an aggregate reflection inside the group. Tending to the group and the worldwide crowd from mission control, she recognizes the significance of moving toward the obscure with modesty and moral care. Dr. Hayes stresses the requirement for mindful investigation that regards the expected presence of extraterrestrial living things and jelly the uprightness of Titan's novel climate.

The moral discussions arrive at a peak as the Titan Explorer moves toward the Deep Door, a baffling submerged passage direct driving toward unfamiliar profundities. The elevated expectation and potential for notable disclosures escalate the moral contemplations. Dr. Victoria Hayes, remaining at the convergence of logical desire and moral obligation, directs the group through extreme conversations about the ramifications of passing this vast boundary.

Commandant James Mitchell, presently confronted with the unmistakable possibility of wandering into the obscure through the Deep Entryway, turns into a voice of wariness in the moral discussions. The likely effect on extraterrestrial biological systems and the sensitive equilibrium of life inside Titan's subsurface sea weigh vigorously on his moral contemplations. The team, isolated in their points of view, takes part in extraordinary exchanges about the moral limits of human investigation in the astronomical outskirts.

Dr. Hayden Carter, upholding for the significance of logical disclosure, winds up definitely having some issues as the impetus framework stands ready for activity.

The moral ramifications of changing the climate for investigation brief soul-looking through conversations inside the group.

Dr. Carter wrestles with the obligation to limit the expected natural effect while pushing the limits of logical information.

Dr. Emily Chang, focused on land investigation, turns into a focal figure in the moral conversations about saving the regular province of Titan's subsurface climate. The land ponders uncovered by the high-goal pictures make a strain between logical interest and the moral obligation to limit obstruction. Dr. Chang, exploring through these moral waters, highlights the significance of moving toward the obscure with worship and restriction.

The natural investigation, catching looks at remarkable living things through specific cameras, elevates the moral intricacy of the mission. Dr. Marcus Thompson turns into a vocal backer for moral rules that focus on the conservation of possible extraterrestrial environments. The discussions increase as the group wrestles with the ethical obligation to stay away from mischief to conceivable life structures while chasing after the logical goals of the mission.

Dr. Alan Rodriguez, directing the arrangement of the mechanical arms, faces moral situations as the group considers connections inside the Deep Door. The expected effect on obscure living things brings up moral issues about the degree to which humankind ought to mediate in the normal request of an extraterrestrial climate. Dr. Rodriguez, exploring through the moral subtleties, underscores the requirement for careful investigation that regards the expected presence of life in Titan's subsurface sea.

Dr. Sophia Ramirez, overseeing correspondence, turns into a conductor for the moral discussions that resound between the shuttle and Earth. The worldwide crowd, presently sensitive to the moral elements of the Titan Explorer mission, participates in conversations about the obligations of humankind as stewards of the universe. Dr. Ramirez, cultivating straightforwardness and moral discourse, turns into a critical figure in forming the public story encompassing the moral contemplations of the mission.

In the last venture of this grandiose show, as the Titan Explorer explores through the Deep Passage, the moral discussions become a characterizing component of the story. Dr. Victoria Hayes, tending to the world from mission control, considers the moral excursion of the group and the aggregate liability to move toward the obscure with veneration and modesty. The moral contemplations become a tradition of the Titan Explorer mission, molding the fate of grandiose investigation and mankind's relationship with the universe.

8.3 The decision to explore the gateway and the potential consequences.

As the Titan Explorer drifts at the limit of the Deep Door, a significant snapshot of choice unfurls, embodying the pith of mankind's unquenchable mission for information and the significant obligation that accompanies wandering into unfamiliar regions.

Dr. Victoria Hayes, the shrewd pioneer directing the mission, remains at the intersection of logical interest and moral contemplations, as the group mulls over the choice to investigate the entryway and wrestles with the potential results that might follow.

Commandant James Mitchell, endowed with the steerage of the Titan Explorer, encounters a snapshot of extraordinary thought. The choice to investigate the Deep Entryway isn't trifled with, as the obscure profundities past coax with the commitment of logical disclosures. Authority Mitchell, mindful of the possible results, ponders the moral components of the excursion and the obligation to explore the unfamiliar waters of Titan's subsurface sea with accuracy and regard.

Dr. Hayden Carter, directing the impetus framework, assumes a basic part in the dynamic cycle. The drive framework, an innovative wonder intended for versatility, stands prepared to impel the Titan Explorer into the obscure profundities past the passage. Dr. Carter, with a sharp consciousness of the possible natural effect, participates in nuanced conversations about the ramifications of enacting the impetus framework and the moral contemplations that go with the choice.

Dr. Emily Chang, the geologist, submerges herself in the high-goal pictures uncovering the geographical miracles inside the Deep Passage. The choice to investigate these unknown areas becomes interlaced with the moral obligation to save the regular territory of Titan's subsurface climate. Dr. Chang, as an overseer of topographical information, advocates for a deliberate methodology that offsets logical interest with a significant regard for the extraterrestrial biological systems that might lie past.

The idea of natural investigation presents a layer of moral intricacy to the dynamic cycle. Dr. Marcus Thompson, managing the organic investigation, thinks about the expected revelation of life structures past the passage. The choice to send specific cameras and possibly experience obscure living things brings up moral issues about the outcomes of human investigation on extraterrestrial environments. Dr. Thompson turns into a voice of wariness, underscoring the moral basic to keep away from hurt while chasing after logical information.

Dr. Alan Rodriguez, organizing the arrangement of the automated arms, ends up at the very front of the dynamic interaction. The mechanical arms, flexible instruments intended for accuracy moves, hold the way to collaborations inside the Deep Entryway. Dr. Rodriguez, mindful of the expected outcomes of conveying the automated arms, participates in conversations about the moral limits of human mediation in an extraterrestrial climate. The choice to initiate the mechanical arms turns into a fragile harmony between logical investigation and moral limitation.

Dr. Sophia Ramirez, overseeing correspondence at mission control, turns into a conductor for the considerations reverberating between the space apparatus and Earth. The choice to investigate the Deep Entryway catches the consideration of the worldwide crowd, igniting conversations about the obligations of humankind as stewards of the universe. Dr. Ramirez, with a guarantee to straightforwardness, guarantees that the moral contemplations and likely outcomes of the choice are conveyed to the world.

As the group discusses the choice, Dr. Victoria Hayes expects the job of a smart go between, exploring through the moral intricacies and possible outcomes. Tending to the group and the worldwide crowd from mission control, Dr. Hayes stresses the heaviness of the choice and the aggregate liability to move toward the obscure with insight and moral care. The choice to investigate the Deep Door, she highlights, is a demonstration of humankind's persistent quest for information yet accompanies the commitment to safeguard and safeguard the infinite conditions they experience.

The choice is made. The Titan Explorer enacts its drive framework, pushing itself into the Deep Door with a deliberate and determined accuracy. As the space apparatus goes through the entryway, the group observers the unfurling marvels of a neglected domain, caught by high-goal pictures and sent to mission control. The choice to investigate the door turns into a groundbreaking second in the story of Sub Stories Titan's Maritime Investigation.

The possible outcomes of the choice become evident as the group explores through the obscure profundities past the entryway. Authority James Mitchell, managing the shuttle's route, experiences varieties in pressure and unfamiliar land highlights. The choice to investigate accompanies difficulties that test the versatility and flexibility of the Titan Explorer. The outcomes of wandering into the obscure become substantial, highlighting the intricacies intrinsic in enormous investigation.

Dr. Hayden Carter, observing the impetus framework, surveys its exhibition continuously as the Titan Explorer ventures into unfamiliar regions. The choice to actuate the impetus framework unfurls with potential natural outcomes that reverberation through the subsurface expanse of Titan. Dr. Carter, cautious in his job, wrestles with the outcomes of modifying the extraterrestrial climate and explores the moral ramifications of the choice.

Dr. Emily Chang, examining geographical information, experiences amazing scenes inside the profundities past the door. The choice to investigate the obscure geographical miracles brings both logical experiences and moral contemplations. Dr. Chang, with a feeling of stunningness and obligation, considers the results of human mediation in these extraterrestrial scenes, aware of the effect that logical investigation might have on the immaculate geographical developments.

The natural investigation uncovers exceptional living things through particular cameras, bringing the likely results of the choice to the very front. Dr. Marcus Thompson, deciphering the organic information, explores through the moral subtleties of experiencing obscure living things. The results of investigating the Deep Passage reach out past logical revelation, molding the moral story of human associations with extraterrestrial environments.

Dr. Alan Rodriguez, sending the mechanical arms with accuracy, experiences expected results as the group gathers tests and leads examinations inside the obscure profundities. The choice to initiate the mechanical arms turns into a sensitive dance between logical request and moral obligation. Dr. Rodriguez, coordinating these perplexing moves, wrestles with the results of human mediation in a climate that has stayed immaculate for ages.

Dr. Sophia Ramirez, overseeing correspondence, turns into a narrator as she sends the outcomes of the choice to investigate the Deep Entryway to the worldwide crowd. The moral contemplations, challenges confronted, and the likely effect on extraterrestrial environments become piece of the account imparted to the world. Dr. Ramirez, with a guarantee to straightforwardness, guarantees that the results of the choice are spoken with clearness and obligation.

Amidst exploring the results, Dr. Victoria Hayes arises as a directing presence, giving knowledge and point of view. Tending to the group and the world from mission control, Dr. Hayes recognizes the difficulties confronted and the possible effect of the choice to investigate. The outcomes, she stresses, are a necessary piece of the investigation account, helping humankind to remember the complicated dance among interest and moral obligation in the enormous unexplored world.

As the Titan Explorer proceeds with its excursion past the Deep Door, the outcomes of the choice unfurl as a unique interchange of logical disclosure, moral contemplations, and the strength of human investigation. The likely effect on extraterrestrial biological systems, the modifications to the regular habitat, and the difficulties looked by the shuttle become strings in the advancing account of Sub Stories Titan's Maritime Investigation.

Chapter 9

Beyond the Abyss

Past the Void, the Titan Explorer leaves on a heavenly odyssey into unfamiliar profundities that rise above the known limits of Titan's subsurface sea. As the shuttle adventures further into the infinite obscure, the story unfurls with layers of logical disclosure, moral contemplations, and unanticipated difficulties, creating an adventure that catches the pith of humankind's quest for information in the midst of the secrets of the universe.

Dr. Victoria Hayes, the visionary chief organizing the mission, remains in charge as the Titan Explorer explores the neglected regions past the Deep Door. Her consistent direction, a reference point in the vast haziness, encourages a feeling of solidarity and reason among the different group of researchers, specialists, and wayfarers. The choice to dig past the Chasm turns into a demonstration of human interest and the aggregate liability to investigate with deference and insight.

Leader James Mitchell, depended with the exact route of the Titan Explorer, experiences an enormous embroidery that resists natural creative mind. Past the Void, the subsurface expanse of Titan uncovers hypnotizing topographical arrangements and complex elements.

The high-goal pictures caught by cutting edge sensors become a visual ensemble of extraterrestrial scenes, inciting wonderment and logical interest. Leader Mitchell, seeing these inestimable marvels, turns into a channel between the obscure and the human soul longing for investigation.

Dr. Hayden Carter, managing the impetus framework, assumes a crucial part as the Titan Explorer diagrams its course through the neglected profundities. The drive framework, adjusted for versatility, pushes the space apparatus with accuracy, winding through the enormous flows of Titan's subsurface sea. Dr. Carter, exploring the sensitive harmony between impetus proficiency and ecological effect, turns into a watchman of the extraterrestrial environment, guaranteeing that the vast excursion leaves negligible follows afterward.

Dr. Emily Chang, the geologist, drenches herself in the geographical wonders revealed past the Pit. The Titan Explorer's investigation uncovers transcending arrangements, geographical delineations, and the multifaceted dance of structural cycles underneath the frosty outside. Dr. Chang, with topographical mastery sharpened on The planet, turns into a trailblazer in translating the outsider geography of Titan, unwinding the grandiose history scratched into its subsurface sea.

Natural investigation past the Void presents Dr. Marcus Thompson to a domain overflowing with expected extraterrestrial life. Particular cameras catch looks at special living things adjusted to the outrageous states of Titan's sea profundities. Dr. Thompson, at the front of natural disclosure, directs the group through moral contemplations, guaranteeing that logical investigation blends with the conservation of outsider biological systems. The journey for life past Earth turns into an unfurling account that enraptures the worldwide creative mind.

Dr. Alan Rodriguez, arranging the arrangement of the mechanical arms, turns into the modeler of complex communications with the grandiose unexplored world. Past the Void, the mechanical arms expand mankind's venture into unfamiliar domains, gathering tests and leading examinations with exceptional accuracy. Dr. Rodriguez, using mechanical ability, opens the mysteries concealed in the extraterrestrial profundities, adding to the developing mosaic of Titan's maritime investigation.

Dr. Sophia Ramirez, overseeing correspondence at mission control, turns into a narrator as the Titan Explorer communicates its inestimable disclosures to Earth. Past the Chasm, the correspondence interface turns into a life saver interfacing the group's excursion with the worldwide crowd. Dr. Ramirez, with editorial artfulness, portrays the unfurling inestimable show, conveying the logical disclosures, moral contemplations, and the close to home ups and downs of the astronomical odyssey.

As the Titan Explorer progresses past the Chasm, the story strengthens with startling difficulties that test the flexibility of both the rocket and its team. Administrator James Mitchell, exploring through unfamiliar regions, faces varieties in pressure, unexpected land highlights, and grandiose flows that request deft changes in the rocket's direction. The difficulties become a cauldron, manufacturing a bond among the group as they stand up to the grandiose obscure sincerely and flexibility.

Dr. Victoria Hayes, recognizing the difficulties experienced past the Void, arises as a wellspring of motivation and direction. Her initiative turns into a steadying power as the group wrestles with the complexities of extraterrestrial investigation. Dr. Hayes, with a significant comprehension of the human soul, encourages a culture of versatility and fellowship, changing difficulties into open doors for logical disclosure and self-improvement.

Dr. Hayden Carter, checking the impetus framework, turns into an investigator as surprising grandiose flows test the flexibility of the Titan Explorer. Past the Void, Dr. Carter's skill in drive elements becomes instrumental in exploring the rocket through the astronomical flows, guaranteeing that the impetus framework answers with accuracy to the always moving divine scene.

Dr. Emily Chang, deciphering geographical information, experiences unexpected topographical highlights that challenge existing logical standards. Past the Pit, the geographical marvels become mysteries that welcome logical request and examination. Dr. Chang, with immovable interest, drives the group in unraveling the extraterrestrial topographical riddles, extending's comprehension humankind might interpret the enormous embroidery woven underneath Titan's frigid surface.

The organic investigation past the Chasm brings Dr. Marcus Thompson up close and personal with the unforeseen variety of extraterrestrial life. Exceptional creatures, adjusted to the outrageous states of Titan's subsurface sea, charm the creative mind of the group. Dr. Thompson, in the midst of the natural disclosures, turns into a promoter for the protection of extraterrestrial biological systems, encouraging mindfulness even with recently discovered life shapes that reclassify the limits of what is known.

Dr. Alan Rodriguez, organizing moves with the automated arms, experiences specialized difficulties past the Pit. The outsider climate presents unexpected snags that request continuous changes in the activity of the mechanical arms. Dr. Rodriguez, with a mix of specialized insight and imaginative critical thinking, guarantees that the mechanical arms explore through the grandiose obscure with accuracy, gathering tests and leading examinations that add to the consistently extending logical story.

Dr. Sophia Ramirez, overseeing correspondence, turns into a channel for communicating the difficulties and wins of the Titan Explorer's infinite process to a worldwide crowd. Past the Void, the correspondence connect turns into a channel for imparting the complexities of extraterrestrial investigation to the world. Dr. Ramirez, with editorial expert articulation, imparts the logical forward leaps, moral contemplations, and the human show of wandering past the known boondocks of Titan.

As the Titan Explorer advances past the Pit, the logical revelations become progressively significant, reshaping's comprehension mankind might interpret Titan's subsurface sea. Leader James Mitchell, with a fantastic view to the enormous exhibition, witnesses land developments that challenge traditional models of planetary geography. The high-goal pictures communicated to mission control become a visual demonstration of the boundless marvels concealed underneath the cold outside of Saturn's biggest moon.

Dr. Victoria Hayes, pondering the unfurling vast show, addresses the worldwide crowd with a message of trust and disclosure. Past the Void, she expresses the meaning of mankind's endeavor into the extraterrestrial obscure, stressing the groundbreaking force of logical investigation. Dr. Hayes turns into an image of visionary initiative, directing humankind towards a future where the infinite obscure coaxes with the commitment of interminable disclosure.

The Titan Explorer, moved by the collaboration of human inventiveness and grandiose versatility, proceeds with its odyssey into strange profundities. Past the Chasm, the shuttle turns into an image of humankind's enduring soul to investigate, adjust, and flourish despite enormous secrets. The excursion, filled by logical interest and moral care, turns into a signal that rises above public lines, motivating people in the future to push the limits of enormous investigation.

In the closing demonstration of this enormous legendary, the Titan Explorer gets back from its odyssey past the Pit, bearing a stash of logical information, moral reflections, and stories of flexibility. Dr. Victoria Hayes, tending to the world from mission control, welcomes mankind to partake in the victories and difficulties of the enormous excursion. Past the Pit, the story turns into a heritage scratched in the chronicles of human investigation, a demonstration of the unyielding soul that moves mankind towards the grandiose unexplored world.

9.1 The team ventures beyond the abyssal gateway into unexplored regions of Titan's ocean.

As the Titan Explorer explores past the Deep Entryway, the group leaves on an earth shattering excursion into unknown districts of Titan's subsurface sea, denoting a significant section in the story of Sub Stories Titan's Maritime Investigation.

Dr. Victoria Hayes, the visionary head of the mission, remains at the front, coordinating the following period of investigation with a sensitive equilibrium of logical interest, moral contemplations, and a feeling of stunningness for the vast unexplored world.

Leader James Mitchell, depended with the steerage of the Titan Explorer, controls the rocket through the astronomical flows past the Deep Door. The once-natural scenes respect the secrets of Titan's neglected sea profundities. Officer Mitchell, a carefully prepared pilot, directs the shuttle with accuracy, acclimating to the moving divine flows and experiencing geographical developments that resist natural examinations. As the group adventures further, the high-goal pictures caught by cutting edge sensors reveal a dreamlike world underneath the frosty outside of Saturn's biggest moon.

Dr. Hayden Carter, supervising the drive framework, turns into a urgent guide in the unknown domains past the entryway. The drive framework, finely tuned for versatility, pushes the Titan Explorer through the extraterrestrial flows, answering the always changing scene of Titan's subsurface sea. Dr. Carter's skill becomes fundamental as the rocket experiences varieties in strain, temperature, and grandiose geography. The impetus framework, a mechanical wonder, turns into the vessel's life saver as it dives further into the grandiose unexplored world.

Dr. Emily Chang, the geologist, drenches herself in the unfurling topographical miracles past the Deep Door. The high-goal pictures sent by the shuttle's sensors uncover transcending arrangements, topographical definitions, and the unique exchange of structural powers underneath the frigid outside layer. Dr. Chang, with a geologist's sharp eye, deciphers the extraterrestrial scene, sorting out the topographical history scratched into Titan's maritime profundities. The neglected landscapes become a material for logical request, provoking inquiries regarding the moon's grandiose development.

Organic investigation presents Dr. Marcus Thompson to the variety of life that might occupy Titan's subsurface sea. Specific cameras catch looks at one of a kind creatures adjusted to the outrageous states of the extraterrestrial climate. Dr. Thompson, at the front of organic disclosure, explores moral contemplations as the group mulls over communications with potential extraterrestrial living things. The organic investigation turns into a vast safari, uncovering the potential for life past Earth and testing assumptions of tenability in the external scopes of our nearby planet group.

Dr. Alan Rodriguez, organizing the arrangement of the automated arms, turns into a craftsman of investigation in the strange domains. The mechanical arms, expanding mankind's venture into extraterrestrial waters, gather tests, and direct investigations with accuracy. Dr. Rodriguez, at the nexus of innovation and investigation, moves the automated arms through the infinite flows, revealing the substance creations and privileged insights concealed inside Titan's maritime profundities. The mechanical arms become instruments of disclosure, examining the obscure with logical artfulness.

Dr. Sophia Ramirez, overseeing correspondence at mission control, turns into a narrator as the Titan Explorer sends its enormous disclosures to Earth. Past the Deep Entryway, the correspondence connect turns into a conductor for imparting the unfurling story to a worldwide crowd. Dr. Ramirez, with editorial style, portrays the logical forward leaps, moral quandaries, and the human show of wandering into neglected regions. The worldwide local area turns into an observer to humankind's introduction to the inestimable outskirts.

As the group adventures further into Titan's maritime profundities, the story turns into an embroidery woven with logical disclosures and unexpected difficulties. Commandant James Mitchell, exploring the space apparatus through unfamiliar flows, experiences varieties in pressure that test the underlying respectability of the Titan Explorer. The group, versatile notwithstanding enormous difficulties, adjusts to the moving elements of the extraterrestrial sea, exhibiting the dauntless soul of human investigation.

Dr. Victoria Hayes, considering the unfurling venture, turns into a guidepost for the group. Past the Deep Entryway, the unknown domains become a representation for the limitless potential outcomes of vast investigation. Dr. Hayes, with a mix of logical intuition and visionary initiative, cultivates a feeling of solidarity among the different group, underscoring the aggregate liability to investigate with lowliness and regard for the infinite unexplored world.

Dr. Hayden Carter, observing the impetus framework, turns into a watchman of the extraterrestrial environment. Past the Pit, the drive framework turns out to be in excess of a mechanical wonder — it turns into a device for capable investigation. Dr. Carter, receptive to the likely natural effect, guarantees that the impetus framework adjusts to the grandiose flows without disturbing the sensitive equilibrium of Titan's subsurface sea.

Dr. Emily Chang, deciphering land information, turns into a trailblazer in unraveling the topographical puzzles past the Pit. The transcending arrangements, multifaceted delineations, and heavenly scenes challenge existing standards of planetary topography. Dr. Chang, unfazed by the vast intricacies, drives the group in disentangling the land history scratched into Titan's extraterrestrial material, adding to the extending embroidery of information about our planetary group.

The natural investigation, directed by Dr. Marcus Thompson, experiences the startling variety of life past the Deep Entryway. Remarkable living beings, adjusted to the outrageous states of Titan's maritime profundities, dazzle the minds of the group. Dr. Thompson, exploring through the moral contemplations of communicating with potential extraterrestrial living things, turns into a supporter for the preservation of outsider environments. The natural investigation turns into a demonstration of the versatility of life in the most impossible corners of the universe.

Dr. Alan Rodriguez, organizing moves with the automated arms, experiences specialized difficulties past the Chasm. The outsider climate presents unanticipated impediments that request constant changes in the activity of the automated arms. Dr. Rodriguez, with a mix of specialized sharpness and innovative critical thinking, guarantees that the mechanical arms explore through the infinite obscure with accuracy, gathering tests and directing examinations that add to the consistently growing logical story.

Dr. Sophia Ramirez, overseeing correspondence, turns into a reference point of straightforwardness as the Titan Explorer communicates its revelations to Earth. Past the Chasm, the correspondence interface turns out to be in excess of a specialized connection point — it turns into an extension interfacing mankind to the vast odyssey. Dr. Ramirez, with persuasiveness and clearness, imparts the logical disclosures, moral contemplations, and the human show of wandering into neglected domains. The worldwide crowd turns into a necessary piece of the grandiose excursion, partaking in the victories and difficulties of Titan's maritime investigation.

As the group adventures further into Titan's sea, the logical disclosures become progressively significant, reshaping's comprehension humankind might interpret the grandiose embroidered artwork. Leader James Mitchell, seeing land developments that challenge natural examinations, turns into a steward of extraterrestrial information. The high-goal pictures sent to mission control become a visual demonstration of the immeasurability of the universe and the complexities concealed underneath the frosty surface of Saturn's moon.

Dr. Victoria Hayes, tending to the world from mission control, turns into a voice of motivation and reflection. Past the Void, she expresses the meaning of mankind's endeavor into neglected locales, accentuating the groundbreaking force of logical investigation. Dr. Hayes turns into an image of visionary initiative, directing mankind towards a future where the vast obscure coaxes with the commitment of unending disclosure.

The Titan Explorer, moved by the cooperative energy of human resourcefulness and enormous versatility, proceeds with its odyssey into the strange profundities. Past the Pit, the space apparatus turns into an image of humankind's faithful soul to investigate, adjust, and flourish notwithstanding inestimable secrets. The excursion, filled by logical interest and moral care, turns into a guide that rises above public lines, rousing people in the future to push the limits of grandiose investigation.

In the closing demonstration of this enormous legendary, the Titan Explorer gets back from its odyssey past the Chasm, bearing a stash of logical information, moral reflections, and stories of strength. Dr. Victoria Hayes, tending to the world from mission control, welcomes humankind to partake in the victories and difficulties of the grandiose excursion. Past the Void, the story turns into a heritage scratched in the records of human investigation, a demonstration of the unyielding soul that moves mankind towards the grandiose unexplored world.

9.2 A culmination of discoveries, challenges, and the team's ultimate mission objectives.

As the Titan Explorer advances further into the unknown domains of Titan's subsurface sea, the excursion turns into an embroidery woven with a zenith of revelations, unexpected difficulties, and the quest for the group's definitive mission targets. Dr. Victoria Hayes, the keen chief guiding the infinite odyssey, winds up at the nexus of logical interest and the significant obligation that accompanies investigating the secrets of the astronomical unexplored world.

Authority James Mitchell, exploring the rocket through the outsider flows past the Deep Entryway, witnesses the unfurling enormous show. The high-goal pictures caught by cutting edge sensors uncover geographical arrangements that resist earthly correlations. Past the Void, the group's mission to disentangle the insider facts concealed underneath Titan's frigid outside turns into a reverberating achievement, as the geographical marvels exposed before them flash logical interest and esteem for the enormous scenes.

Dr. Hayden Carter, observing the drive framework, turns into a caretaker of the shuttle's respectability as it navigates the divine profundities. Past the Void, the drive framework adjusts to the consistently moving flows, answering with an accuracy that shields both the Titan Explorer and the extraterrestrial climate. Dr. Carter's ability in drive elements becomes instrumental in keeping up with the sensitive harmony among investigation and capable stewardship of the enormous domain.

Dr. Emily Chang, deciphering land information, winds up submerged in the stunning vistas uncovered past the Pit. The defined layers, transcending developments, and divine geology become a land material, recounting the narrative of Titan's vast development. Dr. Chang, with a geologist's enthusiasm, translates the extraterrestrial scenes, adding to mankind's extending information on the geographical complexities etched underneath the frigid outside of Saturn's moon.

Natural investigation, drove by Dr. Marcus Thompson, unfurls as an enamoring story of life past the Deep Entryway. Extraordinary living beings adjusted to the outrageous states of Titan's maritime profundities enrapture the minds of the group. Dr. Thompson, at the very front of natural revelation, explores the moral contemplations of cooperating with extraterrestrial living things. The organic investigation turns into a demonstration of the strength and versatility of life in the vast chasm, testing assumptions of tenability in the external compasses of our planetary group.

Dr. Alan Rodriguez, arranging the arrangement of the automated arms, turns into a modeler of complex collaborations with the grandiose unexplored world. Past the Void, the mechanical arms broaden mankind's span, gathering tests and leading examinations with accuracy. Dr. Rodriguez, at the crossing point of innovation and investigation, opens the mysteries concealed inside Titan's maritime profundities. The mechanical arms, with their fragile moves, become instruments of revelation, adding to the developing logical account.

Dr. Sophia Ramirez, overseeing correspondence, turns into a conductor for sending the enormous odyssey to a worldwide crowd. Past the Chasm, the correspondence connect turns out to be in excess of a specialized connection point — it turns into a scaffold associating humankind to the grandiose journey. Dr. Ramirez, with editorial expert articulation, conveys the logical disclosures, moral contemplations, and the human show of wandering into strange regions. The worldwide crowd turns into a fundamental piece of the enormous excursion, partaking in the victories and difficulties of Titan's maritime investigation.

As the Titan Explorer adventures further, the inestimable account turns out to be progressively significant, reshaping's comprehension mankind might interpret the secrets concealed inside the frosty profundities of Saturn's moon. Leader James Mitchell, seeing geographical developments that resist natural examinations, turns into a steward of extraterrestrial information. The high-goal pictures communicated to mission control become a visual demonstration of the tremendousness of the universe and the complexities concealed underneath Titan's frigid surface.

Dr. Victoria Hayes, tending to the world from mission control, turns into a voice of motivation and reflection. Past the Pit, she expresses the meaning of mankind's endeavor into neglected locales, accentuating the extraordinary force of logical investigation. Dr. Hayes turns into an image of visionary initiative, directing humankind towards a future where the enormous obscure coaxes with the commitment of unending disclosure.

The Titan Explorer, pushed by the cooperative energy of human creativity and grandiose strength, proceeds with its odyssey into the strange profundities. Past the Chasm, the rocket turns into an image of humankind's unfaltering soul to investigate, adjust, and flourish even with enormous secrets. The excursion, filled by logical interest and moral care, turns into a guide that rises above public lines, moving people in the future to push the limits of vast investigation.

In the closing demonstration of this grandiose legendary, the Titan Explorer gets back from its odyssey past the Chasm, bearing a stash of logical information, moral reflections, and stories of flexibility. Dr. Victoria Hayes, tending to the world from mission control, welcomes mankind to partake in the victories and difficulties of the grandiose excursion. Past the Chasm, the story turns into a heritage scratched in the records of human investigation, a demonstration of the unstoppable soul that drives mankind towards the vast unexplored world.

As the Titan Explorer approaches the fulfillment of its central goal targets, the group thinks about the significant disclosures, the unanticipated difficulties, and the general reason that has driven them past the Deep Door. Authority James Mitchell, in charge of the shuttle, thinks about the geographical miracles that have divulged themselves in the outsider scenes of Titan. The high-goal pictures, sent with stunning lucidity, uncover the many-sided dance of geographical powers that shape the moon's subsurface sea. Commandant Mitchell, an observer to the geographical orchestra, recognizes the greatness of the revelations and the job they play in growing's comprehension mankind might interpret planetary development.

Dr. Hayden Carter, checking the drive framework, ponders the flexibility and accuracy that have described the space apparatus' excursion past the Void. The impetus framework, a wonder of designing, has answered the grandiose flows with an artfulness that guarantees both investigation and natural obligation. Dr. Carter, a caretaker of drive elements, appreciates the fragile dance between human resourcefulness and the extraterrestrial climate, perceiving the significance of offsetting logical investigation with moral contemplations.

Dr. Emily Chang, drenched in the topographical complexities of Titan, winds up at the front of unraveling the moon's enormous history. Past the Void, the separated layers and transcending developments become parts in a land epic that rises above earthbound stories. Dr. Chang, with a geologist's energy, wonders about the topographical ponders and considers the ramifications of these disclosures on mankind's more extensive comprehension of planetary cycles.

Natural investigation, arranged by Dr. Marcus Thompson, unfurls as an account of strength and variation in the grandiose void. The novel living things found past the Deep Passage challenge assumptions of tenability and highlight the potential for life in the most far-fetched corners of the universe. Dr. Thompson, a pioneer in organic disclosure, ponders the moral contemplations that have directed the group's connections with extraterrestrial living things, perceiving the sensitive harmony between logical request and the protection of enormous biological systems.

Dr. Alan Rodriguez, organizing moves with the automated arms, remains at the convergence of innovation and vast investigation. Past the Chasm, the mechanical arms have gently explored the extraterrestrial waters, gathering tests and directing examinations with an accuracy that has added to the developing logical story. Dr. Rodriguez, a draftsman of investigation, examines the job of innovation in opening the mysteries concealed inside Titan's maritime profundities and the expected ramifications for future space investigation.

Dr. Sophia Ramirez, overseeing correspondence, turns into a narrator winding around the story of Titan's maritime investigation for a worldwide crowd. Past the Pit, the infinite excursion turns into a common encounter, rising above borders and moving aggregate wonderment. Dr. Ramirez, with editorial artfulness, ponders the worldwide effect of the mission, recognizing the job of correspondence in cultivating a feeling of solidarity and shared wonder as humankind journeys into the enormous unexplored world.

As the group thinks about the summit of disclosures, challenges, and the quest for extreme mission goals, Dr. Victoria Hayes tends to the worldwide crowd with a message of appreciation and reflection. Past the Chasm, she underlines the cooperative soul that has characterized the mission, perceiving the aggregate endeavors of researchers, designers, travelers, and the worldwide local area. Dr. Hayes, a reference point of visionary initiative, imagines a future where the examples gained from Titan's maritime investigation move humankind towards much more prominent inestimable undertakings.

The Titan Explorer, having finished its central goal targets past the Deep Passage, starts its process back to Earth, conveying the abundance of logical information, moral bits of knowledge, and stories of vast investigation. Dr. Victoria Hayes, tending to the world from mission control, turns into an image of the unstoppable human soul that tries to push the limits of information. Past the Pit, the story turns into a demonstration of the force of investigation, the versatility of mankind, and the unfathomable possible that lies in the grandiose profundities of the universe.

9.3 The conclusion of the mission and the impact of Titan's exploration on our understanding of extraterrestrial oceans.

As the Titan Explorer approaches the finish of its earth shattering mission, the enormous odyssey that unfurled past the Deep Entryway arrives at its last venture. Dr. Victoria Hayes, the visionary chief coordinating the investigation of Titan's subsurface sea, remains in charge of an excursion that has reshaped's comprehension humankind might interpret extraterrestrial seas and made a permanent imprint on the chronicles of room investigation.

Leader James Mitchell, directing the Titan Explorer through the inestimable flows past the Deep Passage, witnesses the change from unknown domains to the bring venture back. The high-goal pictures caught by cutting edge sensors record the geographical marvels, perplexing developments, and heavenly scenes that have turned into a demonstration of the special embroidery of Titan's maritime profundities. As the shuttle plans to withdraw from the moon's gravitational hug, Authority Mitchell considers the land disclosures and the significant effect of the mission on mainstream researchers.

Dr. Hayden Carter, checking the impetus framework, manages the shuttle's takeoff from Titan's extraterrestrial waters. Past the Pit, the impetus framework adjusts one last time, pushing the Titan Explorer on its direction back to Earth. Dr. Carter, a caretaker of impetus elements, considers the excursion's ecological effect and the sensitive equilibrium that has been kept up with among investigation and the safeguarding of Titan's vast environment.

Dr. Emily Chang, submerged in the topographical marvels of Titan, winds up mulling over the tradition of the mission. Past the Chasm, the separated layers and transcending developments become sections in a land adventure that difficulties assumptions of planetary development. Dr. Chang, with a geologist's veneration for the infinite embroidery, considers the ramifications of the disclosures for our more extensive comprehension of the geography and elements of extraterrestrial seas.

Organic investigation, arranged by Dr. Marcus Thompson, closes with a store of information about the extraordinary living things occupying Titan's maritime profundities. Past the Chasm, the organic disclosures have expansive ramifications for astrobiology and the potential for life past Earth. Dr. Thompson, a trailblazer in natural revelation, ponders the moral contemplations that have directed the group's collaborations with extraterrestrial living things, perceiving the obligation that accompanies the disclosure of outsider biological systems.

Dr. Alan Rodriguez, organizing moves with the mechanical arms, administers the last assortment of tests from Titan's maritime profundities. Past the Chasm, the mechanical arms, expansions of human interest, have carefully explored the extraterrestrial waters, adding to a logical story that rises above the known limits of room investigation. Dr. Rodriguez, a planner of investigation, thinks about the job of innovation in disentangling the secrets concealed inside Titan's outsider climate.

Dr. Sophia Ramirez, overseeing correspondence, turns into the storyteller of the end as the Titan Explorer gets ready to get back. Past the Pit, the correspondence interface fills in as the course for communicating the vast odyssey to a worldwide crowd. Dr. Ramirez, with editorial artfulness, ponders the effect of the mission on the aggregate creative mind of humankind, highlighting the job of correspondence in encouraging a common feeling of marvel and investigation.

As the Titan Explorer starts its process back to Earth, the group ponders the significant revelations, challenges, and the all-encompassing mission goals that have characterized the inestimable odyssey. Commandant James Mitchell, in charge of the shuttle, looks at the subsiding picture of Titan on the survey screens. Past the Pit, the land ponders become a visual memory scratched in the rocket's sensors, a demonstration of the logical accomplishments that have extended's comprehension mankind might interpret the nearby planet group.

Dr. Victoria Hayes, tending to the group and the worldwide crowd from mission control, turns into the voice of reflection and appreciation. Past the Pit, she recognizes the cooperative soul that has characterized the mission and the resolute endeavors of researchers, architects, and pioneers who have wandered into the grandiose unexplored world. Dr. Hayes, an image of visionary administration, expresses the meaning of Titan's investigation in pushing the limits of human information and motivating people in the future to investigate the secrets of the universe.

The Titan Explorer, impelled by the cooperative energy of human inventiveness and inestimable strength, leaves on its return process as the group ponders the effect of Titan's investigation on how we might interpret extraterrestrial seas. Past the Pit, the shuttle turns into a vessel conveying logical information as well as the aggregate goals and dreams of humankind to dig into the secrets of the universe.

In the finishing up demonstration of this grandiose legendary, the Titan Explorer reenters Earth's environment, proclaiming the finish of a noteworthy mission. Dr. Victoria Hayes, tending to the world from mission control, turns into an image of the victorious soul that goes with the arrival of the rocket. Past the Chasm, the story turns into a heritage carved in the texture of human accomplishment, a demonstration of the voracious interest that drives mankind to investigate the unexplored world.

As the Titan Explorer lands on The planet, the group reunites to praise the effective finish of the mission. Administrator James Mitchell, Dr. Hayden Carter, Dr. Emily Chang, Dr. Marcus Thompson, Dr. Alan Rodriguez, and Dr. Sophia Ramirez stand together, addressing the aggregate endeavors that have characterized Titan's investigation. Past the Void, the group turns into a demonstration of the force of joint effort, strength, and the quest for information notwithstanding vast difficulties.

Dr. Victoria Hayes, in a last location to the worldwide crowd, considers the effect of Titan's investigation on how we might interpret extraterrestrial seas. Past the Void, she highlights the extraordinary idea of logical revelation, stressing how Titan's maritime investigation has extended the wildernesses of astrobiology, planetary geography, and the quest for life past Earth. Dr. Hayes turns into a guide of motivation, welcoming humankind to proceed with the excursion of investigation and revelation that stretches past the limits of our home planet.

The Titan Explorer, having finished its main goal targets and got back from the infinite odyssey, turns into an image of human accomplishment and the tenacious quest for information. Past the Pit, the rocket turns into a vessel conveying logical information as well as the aggregate yearnings and dreams of humankind to dig into the secrets of the universe.